PANAMENIAN STREET SPANISH

by

Timothy P. Banse

"Good Books Are Where We Find Our Dreams"

Iowa City, Iowa

Panamanian Street Spanish

Words and Phrases You May Hear in Panama But Won't Find in Your Spanish Language Dictionary.

First Edition - © Copyright 2022

ISBN 978-0-934523-43-1
editor@Middle-Coast-Publishing.com

Publisher's Cataloging- in-Publication data

Banse, Timothy P.
Panamanian Slang : Words and Phrases You Will Hear in Panama But Won't Find in Your Spanish Language Dictionary / by Timothy P. Banse.
pages cm
Includes Index
ISBN 978- 0- 934523- 43- 1
1. Spanish language- - Dialects- - Panama- - Dictionaries. 2. Spanish language- - Provincialisms- - Panama. I. Title.
PC4844.P3
467/.97287 - - dc23   2022PCN

No part of this publication may be reproduced, stored in a retrieval system or transmitted in any form or by any means, electronic, mechanical, photocopying, recording, scanning or otherwise, except as permitted under Sections 107 or 108 of the 1976 U.S. Copyright Act without the prior written permission of the Publisher.

This book is dedicated
to my daughter,

Jessica Marie Larsen

Contents

Origins of Panamanian Spanish	1
Panama's American English Origins	2
Panamanian Versus Textbook Spanish	5
Situations and Conversations	8
Food and Beverage	9
Spices & Vegetables	9
Typical Panamanian Cuisine	11
Main dishes	15
Desserts	18
Chicken	19
Pork	19
Beef	20
Seafood	21
Beverages	22
Adult Beverages	22
Insults	23
Sexuality and Gender	24
Music	25
GLBT	26
Party Time	27
Recreational Drugs	28
Verbs	31
Figures of Speech	43
Dictionary	63
Panamanian Versus Textbook Spanish	123
El Panameño No Dice	123
Verbos	127
Figuras Retóricas	129
About the Author	131

Pronunciation Tips

Practice dropping the letter-S on words ending in, well, S. For example, vamos becomes vamo' (let's go"). Similarly, exchange the ending - ado with - ao. For instance, *cuidado* becomes *cuidao* (be careful). The letters C + Z are pronounced as an S.

The Origins of Panamanian Spanish

For its author, it could be said that this book has been a work in progress since he first arrived on the Isthmus in 1971. Its true genesis dates 500-years even further back to Cristoforo Colon's fourth and final voyage of discovery to the New World when he landed on the shores of Almirante Bay, Panama, on October 16, 1502. Suffice it to say, no matter the date of origin, this title remains a work in progress as Panamanian idioms evolve.

Panamanians will be the first to proclaim that they speak *Castellano* (Castilian), the purest form of the Spanish language. That said, over the past 500-odd years, the Panamanian dialect has absorbed a significant part of its vocabulary from other languages. For example, American English from the Panama Canal Zone. And in addition to English, Panamanian Spanish has also borrowed words from the languages of its many immigrants to the Isthmus, most notably: Africans, French, Italians, Greeks, Chinese (Hakka and Cantonese), and both Hindi and Gujarati East Indians. Also important to note: Contemporary Panamanian Spanish coexists with 19 other languages, including indigenous *Bugle, Ngäbere, Embera, Wounaan, Kuna, Naso Tjerdi, Bribri,* and English Creole.

Point of reference: The French were the first to try to dig a Panama Canal. During the 1880s, Frenchman Ferdinand Marie Vicomte de Lesseps, renowned engineer and developer of the Suez Canal, which linked the Mediterranean and Red Seas in 1869, attempted to repeat his success in building a sea-level canal in Panama. But epidemics of malaria and yellow fever devastated the workforce and the project. While the French are long gone, a sprinkling of their words remains. Such as beaucoup, which is just one of the many French words in (Panamanian slang).

Panama's American/English Origins

A moment ago, we mentioned the American Panama Canal. So it should come as no great surprise to learn that lots of Panamanian slanguage (sic) *have its origins in English words.* You probably already know that Yankee adventurers visited Panama in great numbers as early as the 1849 gold rush. Some traveled to the California gold fields overland, some by ship around Cape Horn. Others sailed from the Port of New Orleans to a Panamanian book town called Chagres City, then located at the mouth of the Chagres River near Fort San Lorenzo.

Today the town is long gone, but its ruins can be found behind the jungle treeline at Piñas Beach. To get an idea of the town's size back then, know that during the California Gold Rush (1848–1855), Chagres City was populated with as many as 2,000 prostitutes.

Chagres was a notorious breeding spot for yellow fever, cholera, and malaria. The death rate was so high that most insurance carriers included a clause in their policies stating that all benefits would be canceled automatically should the policyholder remain overnight in the village. No big surprise, 49ers died like flies.

We know from historical accounts that some entrepreneurial booze merchants pickled the dead bodies of men killed by fever in rum and shipped them to New Orleans, where the cadavers were dispatched further onward to medical schools. Those Forty-Niners who survived gunshot wounds, bar brawls, malaria, and yellow fever hired *bongos* (native dugout canoes) to paddle them the 40-some miles up the Chagres River. The passage upriver took about three days with overnight stops at native villages. Food was difficult to find, so they supped on iguana, snakes, monkeys, and other exotic animals.

They disembarked upon reaching either Cruces or Gorgona, where they paid off the boat owners and then negotiated a price for mule transportation the rest of the way to Panama City, 20-miles further on. Ultimately, they booked passage on a clipper ship the rest of the way to San Francisco.

You already know the story of the building of the Panama Canal. Sum and substance, influenced by American English, contemporary

Panamanian lingo tends to rather smoothly co-mingle Spanish with English. For example:

Arabauns - Out of bounds, as when playing American football.

Buay - A boy. *Niño*.

Camarón - From come around, meaning non-permanent work. Not to be confused with *camaron*, or the seafood shrimp.

Birra - A beer.

Blod - Blood. A close friend.

Charcot - From shortcut. A faster route to get to somewhere.

Charcotear - To take a shortcut.

Chingongo - Chewing gum.

Corn Flakes - Cornflakes. Pronounced conflei.

Cuara - A quarter - 25 centavos.

Culei - Kool-Aid.

Daim - A dime. - Ten (10) centavos.

Eslipinbag - A sleeping bag.

Fraslai - Flashlight. *Se pronuncia fraj lait.*

Fren - Means friend, or cool.

Friquiado - Freaked out.

Fuckup/Fokot - Means a fuck up.

Full - Very. Completely. The maximum.

Guaiter - Waiter.

Gualet - Wallet.

Guapin - What's happening.

Guarever - Whatever.

Guial/Gyal - Girl, woman, chick. Used in Colón.

Guichiguaiper - Windshield wiper.

Jorol - Huddle, as when playing American football.

Láiter - Cigarette lighter.

Likibuay - A little boy.

Man - Man.

Naitafón - Night of fun.

Pritty - Means pretty or cool.

Qué power - An 80's term, meaning - That's awesome!

Rilax - Relaxed.

Tu rasssss - Yer ass.

Wapin - Wapin you - From the English phrase: What's happening - *Wapin mi fren*. Often accompanied with an energetic snapping of the first two fingers. You'll know what I mean when you see/hear it.

Yacama - A jackhammer.

Yiyinbré - Ginger bread.

Panamanian Spanish Versus Textbook Spanish

Panamanian lingo often transposes (*traspalantar*) the last two or three letters from the back of a word to the front. For example:

Bezaca is *Cabeza* reversed (head).

Bochon is *Chombo* reversed (black guy).

Breham is *Hambre* reversed (hungry).

Coblan is *Blanco* reversed (white).

Datien is *Tienda* reversed (store).

Gadaca is *Cagada* reversed (shit).

Gandoca - Pooping, letters in reversed order. *Traspalante de cagando (defecar).*

Gogrin is *Gringo* reversed (americano).

Goti is *Contigo* reversed. With you, as in *Xopa con Goti*

Is (pronounced, eess) is *Sí* reversed (Yes).

Laope is *Pelao* reversed (boy).

Lofu is *Fulo* reversed (blond).

Lleca - Calle reversed spelling. *Traspalante derivado de Calle.*

Llesca is *Calle* reversed (street).

Llopo Is *pollo* reversed (chicken.)

Mopri is p*rimo* reversed (cousin).

On is *no* reversed.

Oti Is *tio* reversed (uncle)

Soque is *queso* (cheese) reversed.

Sopi - Is piso is a flat , or apartment.

Sopre Is *preso* reversed (prisoner.)

Tavuel V*uelta* is reversed (To go out).

Temalean is *Maleante* reversed (gangsta).

Tospa is *Pato* reversed (duck).

Xopa - Consider the phrase: *Qué Xopa*, which is *Qué paso* modified. *Paso* becomes *Sopa* when written, wherein the letter X replaces the letter S in order to avoid confusing with *sopa*, the word for soup. Sometimes the expression is shortened to a single word as in: *Xopa*. Qué sopá? - What's up? ¿*Cómo estas?* To which one answers: *Too cul* - Life is good.

Yapla is *Playa* (beach).

Panamanians like to shorten words by omitting the last syllable. For example:

¡Ayala! (sometimes pronounced *'áshala')* - From *Vaya la.* (Express surprise).

Oficial becomes *Ofii* (Okay).

Oseaa is an abbreviation for *Lo qué sea.* (Whatever)

Pa is short for *para. Esto es pa' ti.* This is for you.

Palante From *para adelante.* To go forward, slang for, leave.

Pelan ¡*Pálante!* is shortened.

Que Becomes the single letter **K** (What).

Sae is *Saber* shortened (To know).

Ta is Short for *está* (It is).

' **Toy** *Estoy*. I am there. Count me in.

Panamanians creatively construct verbs out of whole cloth (so to speak) by adding the endings - *ear* or - *iar* to English verbs. It's an ingenious way to create verbs relating to new technologies when the vocabulary is not yet available in the Spanish language. For example:

Chatear - To chat, meaning chatting on the internet.

Chiliar - To chill.

Chopear - To shop.

Clipsar - To staple.

Escanear - To scan a document.

Hanguear - To hang out.

Huevear - To hang out.

Printear - To print.

Typear - To type at a keyboard.

Situations and Conversations

Panamanians respect good manners. So pleasantly greet others with a mannerly choice of words and phrases. And in conversation, be sure to use the polite form of *usted* (you).

Buenos días - Good morning or *Buenas tardes* (good afternoon).

Greeting upon entering a store - ¡*Bueeenas!* (draw out)

At the first sign of a cloud in the sky - ¡*Viene el agua!* (here comes the *agua*/rain.) Panamanians don't say it's raining really hard. Instead *El panameño no dice está lloviendo muy fuerte, dice está cayendo un palo de agua*

¡*Queé va!* - What utter nonsense.

Como no - But of course.

Voy pa alla - I go there.

Noommbe - Contraction of *No hombre*. No way, man.

Esto Ummmm - Begins a sentence.

¡*Qué vaina!* - What a big load of bullshit.

¡*Ayala vida!* - Holy shit (So to speak).

Asi es la vida - That's life! So it goes.

¡*Jo!* - To emphasize a reaction to a shocking revelation.

¡*Chuleta!* - Amazement. See dictionary listing for details.

Food and Beverage

A la parilla – Grilled.

Asada – Roasted.

Comida corriente - Fast food.

Spices and Vegetables

Ajo - Garlic.

Aji - Peppers (like *aji, dulce* are usually the little red, green, and yellow sweet peppers).

Cebolla - Onion.

Culantro - Contrary to what you might think, culantro is not an alternate spelling of cilantro and it's a completely different plant. Although the two cultivars are cousins, they look nothing alike.

Guandú – Pigeon peas. *Guandú* often cooked with rice. Bags of guandú peas are sold in most local market places and a few super markets when in season

Maiz - Corn.

Mamón Chino - A tropical fruit, its green thorny/hairy balls gradually turn red as they ripen over the course of about 6 months. Enjoy the sweet, creamy pulp by popping the whole fruit inside your mouth and sucking on the pulp, all the while being cautious not to swallow the large seed. The juice dyes fabric brown. Also available in jams.

Ñame - A starchy root often used in soups also means someone crazy. Also see *Otoe*. The word is believed to be derived from a West African language like: Fulani, Serer, or Wolof.

Otoe - A flowering plant eaten in soups as a replacement for potatoes. Synonyms: *taro, ñame, dasheen, malanga.*

Papa - Potato.

Pepino - Cucumber.

Pifa o Pixbae - The fruit of a palm tree with the texture of a potato and the savory flavor of a smoked yam. When ripe it is a beautiful red fruit, when immature it is yellowish to green. With nearly the nutritional value of an egg, it is high in protein and contains beta- carotene, phosphorus, Vitamin A, some B and C, calcium and iron. Delicious when cooked, it tastes best when dressed in salt and honey. Called *chontaduro* in other Latin American countries, it is reputed to be a natural aphrodisiac.

Repollo - Cabbage.

Tamarillo - Tree tomato, eaten by scooping the flesh from a halved fruit. Lightly sugared and cooled, the flesh is a breakfast dish. Fresh tamarillos are frequently blended together with water and sugar to make a juice. Tamarillo flesh is tangy and variably sweet and sour to kiwifruit, tomato, guava, or passion fruit. The skin is bitter tasting and the fruit is not usually eaten raw

Tomate - Tomato.

Zapayo - Squash.

Typical Panamanian Cuisine

Panamanian cuisine is a unique mix of many of the world's cultures including African, Spanish and indigenous. Typical foods are mildly flavored and common ingredients include maize, rice, wheat flour, plantains, yuca (cassava), beef, chicken, pork and seafood. Many Panamanian dishes are made from corn, but interesting to note, the preparation is different than other Latin American corn dishes, this includes corn tortillas and arepas. In Panama the kernel is first cooked in water and then ground in order to create dough while in other Latin American cooking the dough is made from corn flour. Fresh corn is also used in some dishes. Here is an overview of some specialties:

Almojábanos - S- shaped corn fritters.

Bollos - Corn dough wrapped in corn husk or plantain leaves and boiled. There are two main varieties: fresh corn *bollos* (*bollos de maíz nuevo*) and dry corn *bollos*. The dry corn type is sometimes flavored with butter, corn, or stuffed with beef, which is called *bollo preñado*.

Carimañola - Similar to an *empanada*, only made from yuca and stuffed with beef. Panamanian/Colombian meat- pie shaped in a torpedo- shaped yuca fritter, stuffed with cheese, seasoned ground meat or shredded chicken and then fried. Carimañola are made with ground beef (*piccadillo*) and never with iguana, racoon (*gato solo*) or chicken. They are fried, never baked.

Chifles: Thinly sliced chips, like potato chips, now being but also also made from yucca/cassava. These potato like chips have an infinite number of flavoring possibilities.

Chiswiz - A snack like Doritos, Tostitos. Derived from Cheez Whiz, the thick, processed cheese spread sold by Kraft Foods. *Una merienda*.

Chupata - A gathering of friends and neighbours.

Cicsa - A fast drink, but it can also mean a lame product

Con colón - Crusty rice burned in the bottom of pan. The origin of this figure of speech is said to be from the sailors who accompanied Cristobal Colon (aka Christopher Columbus) on his four voyages to the New World. To eat *Concolón* was to dine with the captain, who traditionally ate only after his crew had been fed, or literally, con Colón. In Valencia, Spain, the encrusted rice in the bottom of a paella pan is called *socarrat*, derived from the verb *socarrar* meaning to burn, or to toast.

Conflei - See corn Flakes.

Cornflake - Any kind of dry breakfast cereal. *Quiero comer cornflake.* I want to eat cereal.

Croquetas de Yucca - See *Carimañola*.

Dulce - Cake. Let them eat cake.

Dulce de leche - Caramelized condensed milk.

Empanada - A fried flour or corn pastry stuffed with ground beef or other meats and cheeses. It's called a patty on the Caribbean side.

Empanadas - Made from either flour or corn meal and stuffed with meat, cheese and sometimes sweet fillings, like fruit marmalade or *manjar blanco (dulce de leche)*.

Fonda - A small restaurant serving traditional Panamanian food with a limited number of *entreés.* Meals are inexpensive and the food is served promptly.

Hojaldres/Hojaldras - Fry- bread similar to South American *sopaipilla.*

Huevos - Hen eggs. Never ask a butter and egg man if has eggs. Instead, ask if there are any eggs: e.g. *¿Hay huevos?* Asking if he has eggs (*¿Tiene huevos?*) is to ask, "Do you have balls (testicles)?"

Keke - Cake. A sweet treat made with flour, shredded coconut and honey. Also see: *Queque, un dulce horneado que se prepara con harina, coco rayada y miel.*

Macaron or Macaroni - Pasta or spaghetti.

Meneito - Cheese chips. Alternatively a song by Gaby. Also shaking your tail feathers (butt).

Mondungo - A dish made from only the first three chambers of a cow's stomach. ie Tripe. Spelled *mundungo* in rural Panama. With their arrival for the building of the trans- isthmian railroad, the Chinese taught the Panamanians how to clean and process this food. Panamanian *mondongo* is different than other countries. Here, unlike other Latin American countries, it is not prepared as a soup, but instead more like a stew and served with white rice, or rice with green pigeon peas. Mondongo *a la Culona* (Big Butt Woman's Style), is prepared with pigs feet and tails.

Morrina - Rotten dog food, also describes any rotten food.

Pankeke - Pancake.

Patacón/Patacónes - Green plantain slices squashed into a patty and fried until golden brown, then removed from heat then smashed with your hand or in a wooden press called a *tostonera* that produces a flattened, or basket *Pionono/Canasta*. Requires a hard, green, plantain which is why it is pressed it after frying and then refried. Eat with a spritz of fresh lime juice and a sprinkle of cayenne pepper. Alternatively known in other countries as *Tostones. Rodajas de plátano aplastadas y fritas.*

Patty - On the Caribbean side of the isthmus an empanada is called a patty.

Pebre - Food. *Comida*.

Plantanos maduro - Ripe, spears fried until they caramelize, sometimes first or sprinkled with sugar to speed and the process.

Platanos tentacion - Baked green plantains typically candied with local sugar and sometimes the spices: rum, allspice, cinnamon and vanilla or fruit (for the temptation). Some recipes use juice or Coke or orange soda as a secret ingredient.

Platanos tirades - Sliced length ways then fried.

Platanaos canoas - Full length and halved, then stuffed either sweet or savory ingredients.

Plantanitos - Fried plantain chips.

Plantintá - A plantain tart. An *empanada* made with plantain stuffed inside.

Porcambín - Pork and beans.

Porcón - Pop corn.

Raspao - An American carnival- style snow cone, which is to say a paper cone filled with crushed ice and flavored by colorful, fruity, sweet syrups.

Sancocho Chiricano - A specialty from Chiriquí Province, this is the heartiest variety of *sancocho,* containing squash which lends the meal a yellowish tint. In addition to all basic and optional ingredients previously mentioned. It is both recommended as a potent hangover remedy and also a metaphor for the Panama's racial diversity, thanks to the varied list of ingredients.

Sancocho Chorrerano - A specialty of the town of La Chorrera, where it's made with free range chicken, onions, garlic, chili peppers, oregano and of course, *ñame*.

Sancocho de gallina - From the Spanish verb *sancochar* (To parboil). The national dish of Panama originates from the Azuero region and its basic ingredients include free range chicken *ñame*, for flavor and as a thickener, lends this soup or stew its characteristic texture and brightness *culantro* (gives its characteristic flavor and greenish tone) *yuca, mazorca* (Corn on the cob) and *otoe* are also added. Optional ingredients include *ñampí* (the Eddoe variety of Taro), chopped onions, garlic and oregano. It's frequently served with white rice on the side, meant to be either mixed in or eaten with each spoonful. Hot sauce is added, depending on regional and individual preferences.

Seviche - Ceviche - Cebiche - Fresh raw seafood marinated in lemon or lime juice and spiced with chopped onion, celery, *habanero* pepper and sea salt. *Besides Ceviche de corvina* (white sea bass), served as an appetizer in many restaurants, *seviche* is also made with octopus, shrimp and squid. Important to know: In addition to flavoring, the citric acid denatures the proteins, changing the appearance and texture of the chunks of fish.

Be advised, and contrary to what you will hear, Seviche is NOT cooked! Therefore, bacteria and parasites are not killed.

Prepare fresh to minimize the risk of food poisoning, safer yet, prepare with frozen or blast- frozen fish due. Raw seafood, which *Seviche* is, can be the vector for various pathogens, viral, bacterial, as well as larger parasitic creatures. Specific microbial hazards in *ceviche* include: *Anisakis simplex, Diphyllobothrium spp., Pseudoterranova decipiens, and Vibrio parahaemolyticus.*

Tortilla - Called an *Arepa* by Venezuelans and Colombians.

Torrejitas de maíz - A *Fritura*, a fresh corn fritter.

Tortillas – Ten- to 12-inches in diameter and cooked on a griddle.

Tortilla changa - Thick tortilla made out of fresh corn.

Totopos - Tortilla chips (corn).

Tuti- fruti - Canned fruit cocktail often served in Jell-O and at birthday parties. In the U.S. Midwest we find the equivalent in the ubiquitous fruit-flavored Jell-O mold populated with marshmallows, bananas, or Mandarin oranges and sometimes even chunked hot dogs.

Main Dishes

Arroz con bacalao - Rice with cod fish.

Arroz con chorizo y ajíes dulces - Rice with sausage and sweet peppers.

Arroz con guandü - Rice with pigeon peas.

Arroz con mollejas - Rice with gizzards. Dirty rice in Louisiana.

Arroz con pollo - Chicken and rice.

Arroz con puerco y vegetales - Rice with pork and vegetables.

Arroz con sombrero - A plate of rice with a fried egg on top. Rice with a hat.

Arroz con tities y coco - Rice with tiny "popcorn" shrimp and coconut milk.

Arroz verde - Green rice (Spinach and cilantro).

Bistec de hígado - Liver steak.

Bistec picado - Chopped beefsteak.

Bistec entero - A braised Swiss steak.

Carne entomatada - Meat cooked in tomato sauce.

Ceviche - Commonly made from *corvina (See Seviche)*.

Chorizo con vegetales - Sausage with vegetables.

Chuletas en salsa de piña - Pork chops in pineapple salsa.

Ensalada de papas - Potato salad, called *ensalada de feria,* when beet root is added. Sometimes called Russian salad.

Güacho - Stew/soup with rice, beans and some meat (pork tail). *Plato de arroz cocido con carne y verduras que parece sopa espesa.*

Johnny Mazetti - As the story goes, this Panama Canal Zone favourite originated in the Columbus, Ohio, Marzetti family restaurant. Teresa Marzetti, owner, created this baked casserole dish and named it after her brother in law, Johnny. You may have already guessed this is the same family as the T Marzetti Company famous for its salad dressing. Variations on the recipe's spelling include Marzetti and Marzotti. Ingredients include ground beef, tomatoes, celery, yellow onions, green peppers, and either egg noodles or macaroni. The Zonian version, which had migrated to the isthmus around the time of the Second World War, adds green olives.

Lengua guisada - Stewed beef tongue.

Mondongo a la culona - Stewed beef tripe.

Pernil de pueco al horno - Roasted pork leg.

Plátano en tentacion - Ripe plantain cooked in a sweet syrup.

Salpicón de carne - Shredded beef.

Tamal - Made from sometimes old corn sometimes new corn, and stuffed with pork or chicken. *Delicioso preparado hecho de maíz viejo, con carne de puerco o de gallina. El mismo es envuelto en hoja de tallo. Algunos lo hacen de maíz nuevo*

Tamal de ollaor - Tamale of the pot/pan. Panamanian-style tamale that fills its baking pan. Unlike a conventional tamale, this one is not wrapped in a banana or plantain leaf. Ingredients include pork or chicken cooked with corn- stuffed cornmeal (*maiz nuevo*), vegetables (onion, tomato, and bell pepper), olives, and raisins.

Tasajo - Dried or smoked meat, usually beef, and the word refers mainly to the method of curing rather than the cut of meat.

Desserts – Postres

Bocado de la reina - The *Bocado de Reina* cake made with leftover bread, though it is not bread pudding because its consistency is that of a cake. Literally translated *Bocado de Reina* means Bite of a Queen, carrying the meaning of a food fit for a queen.

Cabanga - A desert made with green papaya, guayaba, and coco milk. *Dulce endurecido que se corta en pedazos rectangulares, hecho con papaya verde, guayaba, coco, canela, leche, raspadura o miel.*

Cocadas - *Cocadas* are a coconut candy or cookie.

Duro - Frozen fruit in a plastic cup. *Refresco de frutas congelado en una bolsita plastic.*

Huevitos de leche' - Decadently delicious eggs of milk (or milk candy) guaranteed to set off a sugar high. Readily available in stores.

Pesada de nance - *Nance* is a sweet, yellow, strongly scented fruit. *Los nances se compran por botellas.* Served as a Chicha or a when cooked with white or brown sugar, evaporated milk and white cheese, its a delicious, traditional, Panamanian desert.

Tres leches - Milk cake. Made with three layers: Cake, filling, and topping with three different types of milk in the filling and topping (whole milk, condensed milk, evaporated milk, and heavy cream).

Chicken - Pollo

Alas de pollo alitas - Chicken wings.

Filete de encuentro de pollo - Boneless thigh. (*Filete* means boneless.

Filete de pechuga - Boneless chicken breast.

Muslo encuentro - Thigh and drumstick.

Muslo de pollo - This is the chicken leg all by itself.

Pechuga de Pollo - This is chicken breast.

Pollo entero - A whole chicken.

Pork - Puerco

Chuleta ahumada - Smoked pork chop.

Chuletas deshuesadas - Boneless pork chops

Chuletas frescas - Pork chops (uncooked).

Costillas de puerco - Pork ribs.

Lomo de cerdo - Pork tenderloin.

Lomo de puerco - Pork tenderloin.

Tocino - Bacon.

Beef - Res

Babilla - Rump steak.

Bistec de centro - Top round steak.

Bistec de filete - Tenderloin steak.

Bistec de lomo - Top loin (strip) steak.

Bistec picado - Steak chopped into little strips for stir-fry.

Bistec de planchuela - Chuck top blade steak.

Bistec suavizado - Cube steak.

Carne para guisar - Stew meat: Either chunked or cubed for soups or stews.

Carne molida - Ground beef.

Carne pulpa negra - Top round, one of the most popular cuts in Panama.

Costillar punta pequeña - Rib roast.

Falda - This is flank steak. *Falda* of course, means skirt.

Filete en trozo - Tenderloin roast.

Lomo redondo - Beef *lomo*, as with pork, is tenderloin.

Milanesa - Thin-cut round steak.

Milanesa de pulpa bola - Round tip steak.

Paleta del 7 en trozo - Chuck 7-Bone pot roast

Paleta en trozo - Chuck arm pot roast

Palomilla - Beef loin sirloin.

Pecho corte - Brisket, flat cut.

Pecho entero - Brisket, whole.

Pulpa blanca - Bottom round.

Pulpa bolo en troza - Round tip roast.

Ropa vieja - Literally translated means old clothes, this is flank steak shredded like pulled pork.

Tiritas de carne - Beef for stir-fry.

Seafood – Mariscos

Corvina - Similar to snapper and sea bass and regarded as a prime table fish also a prime ingredient in *seviche*.

Lisa - Mullet.

Pargo - Snapper. *Huichinango.*

Pargo rojo - Red snapper.

Robalo - Snook.

Sierra - Mackerel, more particularly, Spanish mackerel.

Titties - Small shrimp.

Beverages - Bebidas

Fresh fruit juices (*licuados or jugos naturales*): pineapple, passion fruit, papaya, orange, tree tomato, etc. are prepared by blending fresh fruit and straining, typically heavily sweetened and optionally with condensed milk added.

Atole de maiz - A cornmeal hot drink. A blend of milk, sweet corn or cornmeal, cinnamon, vanilla, and sometimes water. Yum.

Batido de guineo banana - A banana smoothie.

Chicha - Originally the name of an indigenous alcoholic drink made from corn, but in Panama, a generic name for any kind of juice to which water and sugar are added. So, a watered-down fruit juice (*jugo, zumo*). For example: *Eso ta chicha 'e piña* means That's easy. A piece of cake.

Chichas - A class of fruit juice-based beverages including *Chicha Arroz con Piña* (Rice and Pineapple).

Chicheme - A corn-based beverage.

Guarapo (de caña) - A non-alcoholic beverage made from sugar cane.

Resbaladera - Technically Costa Rican, but widely enjoyed here in neighboring Panama, this non-alcoholic chilled grain and milk drink is similar to *chicheme. Horchata.*

Adult Beverages – Bebidas

Bajapanti - Both a popular and cheap wine called Night Train Express and a phrase that quite literally means panty remover.

Chichita Panamá - Mixed drink: Seco, grapefruit & pineapple juice.

Chirrisco - Homebrew alcohol from the rural Panama. Some say the brew is dosed with battery acid to accelerate fermentation.

Fría - Literally, a cold one. A beer. *Una cerveza.*

Guaro - An alcoholic beverage made from fermented guarapo. Sometimes spelled *waro*. *Una beba alcohólica. Licor.*

Nueve letras - Nine letters. Popular name for the best selling brand of Seco in Panama, *Herrerano*, which coincidentally just happens to have nine letters.

Pinta - Beer, as in the ubiquitous pint of beer.

Rompe pecho - A large bottle of beer or soda.

Ron ponche - Rum punch.

Seco - Panama Seco - Seco literally means dry, like a martini. Seco, the national alcoholic beverage of Panama, is triple distilled from sugarcane. An eighty- proof crystal clear liquor taken straight- up or mixed as a replacement for rum or vodka in a cocktail. Seco is mixed with everything from tropical fruit juices, and tonic to milk and coconut milk. See *Chichita Panamá*. Seco Herrerano is the most popular brand of *seco* and brewed by the Herrerano family who invented the spirit in Panama back in 1908.

Seco con vaca - On the Atlantic side of the isthmus, *Seco* is mixed with milk or coconut milk. Literally: *Seco* with cow's milk.

Waro - See *Guaro*.

Insults

Awebao - Derived from the root word *ahuevado*, or egg- headed. The word can either be derogatory and mean idiot, or it can be friendly jib meaning, dude. The difference depends on the tone of voice. Pronunciation varies: *awebado, awebao, aw or aoaooo*. A pussy.

Awebasono - Ahuevason - Things that are foolish or just plain dumb.

Bagre - Literally means a catfish, but in *yerga* it means a really ugly woman. A synonym to *cangreja*.

Bobo - Dumb man or woman. Someone who is particularly foolish.

Cangreja - A female crab, an unattractive woman.

Cara de verga - Dick face.

Chambín - A clumsy oaf.

Chombo - A derogatory term for black people and the rough equivalent of nigger in American English. Please don't use this offensive word.

Chucha de tu madre - Your mother's genitalia.

Cocodrila - Derived from the reptile *cocodrilo*, (crocodile) this word, used as slang, means a particularly ugly woman.

Congo - A person whom is regularly taken advantage of, which is to say, an idiot. The word has nothing to do with the country in Africa.

Culantron - Big ass. From *culo*, the Spanish word for hips/ass.

Culicagao - A moron or a cowardly person. Also, a very young person. See *pelaito*.

Gargola - Gargoyle. A really ugly woman. *Manuelita es mansa gargola*.

Gufi - Goofy. Crazy person, sometimes pronounced as: *bufi*.

Pilinki - A cheapskate, *una persona tacaña*.

¡Tas ahueva! - You egghead, you idiot!

Sexuality and Gender

Arrecho - Sexually excited. Aroused.

Catribolia - A woman who is highly, sexually-charged. The proverbial nymphomaniac.

Chucha - Contrary to popular gringo opinion, this word is NOT necessarily a vulgar reference to the female reproductive organ. Instead, it is used an expression of shock, or surprise, an expression of anger, happiness, surprise, sadness, speechlessness. *¡Chucha! ¡Qué bien me fue! ¡Que chucha! Qué mal me fue. ¡Chucha! No se como me fue. Estoy en chucao.* (I am angry).

¡Coño! - Cunt. Pussy. A somewhat vulgar expression, the actual meaning differs according to use expressing a wide variety of emotions: Fear, anger, surprise, or joy. Used like the word fuck in American English.

Cuatrera - A prostitute.

Culearto - To have carnal knowledge (sex). *El panameño no hace el amor sino: Culea.*

Micha - Panamanians slang for vagina. Also *cuca, araña,* and *tontón*.

Mota - Yet another Panamanians slang word for vagina. In Mexican Spanish the word means marijuana.

Pai - Derived from the American English word: Pie. It means a sexually attractive woman. To better comprehend the concept, in your mind's eye imagine the frontal view of a woman's bikini bottom that resembles a slice of pie as in: *Qué pai*!

Rabo - Dick.

Rochadera - A make out session.

Yeguero - Horsefucker, a sexually desperate person who will have relations with anyone. (*Yegua* = mare)

Music

Plena - The Panamanian version of reggae, but also used for other genres of music when the song is good. *Canciones/ritmos de reggae. DJ pon plena* - DJ play some plena.

Reggaeton - Reggae in Spanish with roots in Latin and Caribbean music. Vocals include rapping and singing, typically in Spanish with hip hop lyrics.

GLBT

Bajito'e sal - Gay. Literally means: Low on salt.

Batea y corre pa tercera - Slang refers to people who are gay or homosexual. Roughly translated this baseball related figure of speech means hits and runs to third base.

BatiBuay - Gay.

Cueco/Cueca - Gay or lesbian. A pejorative term for gay (*cueco*- male) or lesbian (*cueca*).

Maricon - Butterfly, gay.

Mariflor - Gay.

Mariposa - A butterfly.

Mariposo - A gay, differentiated from *mariposa*, which is a butterfly.

Masca bola/ Masca verga - A cock sucker.

Ñaío - Un Gay.

Ñorro - Un Gay.

Pato - Un Gay. Literally, duck.

Revuelve- porotos - Gay

Se le moja la canoa - His canoe is getting wet, or sinking, referring to an effeminate man.

Tortillera - Derogatory term for a lesbian. *Lesbiana*.

Tralalai - Gay.

Welemedia or Soksniffa - Gay. Literally a sock sniffer, a brown-noser, someone who sucks up.

Party Time

El Arranque - 1. One for the road. As in: *Esto es el arranque.* - This is the last drink. 2. - A party. Literally the starting point ¡*Vamos pal arranque!* Let's go to the party!

Canchalarga - A party animal. Someone who can party on forever. It literally means: a long field.

Chupata - A celebration that involves drinking massive quantities of alcohol.

Enculado - To be very much in love, sigh. Especially at the beginning of a relationship. *Estí enculado.*

Estar en fuego - To be drunk.

Goma - A hangover. ¡*Hay, Qué goma tengo!* What a hangover I've have!

Hasta la requite - See *hasta la verga*.

Hasta la verga - To be extremely drunk. Also: *Hasta la zapatillapa, hasta la wacha, hasta la wacharneta, hasta la requete.*

Hasta la wacha - See *hasta la verga*.

Hasta la wacharneta - See *hasta la verga*.

Hasta la zapatilla - See *hasta la verga*.

Jumarse - Often colloquially used instead of *emborracharse* (to get drunk).

Rochadera - A make- out session.

Traigo - A mixed drink, a cocktail. *Dame otra traigo, por favor.*

Recreational Drugs - Las Drogas

Basuco - A contraction of *Basura de la cocaina*, literally, trash from cocaine. A deadly, illegal narcotic that is the residue left over after extracting cocaine base. The residue is a dirty, sticky, and muddy-brown paste that contains a number of toxic chemicals including sulfuric acid. With corrosive acid and other toxins intact, about 1,000 grams of *basuco* can be obtained from a single gram of cocaine. *Basuco* is dried, sold and then smoked. The drug is both toxic and extremely addictive, causing destruction of brain tissue and loss of memory, chemical pneumonitis, pulmonary edema, excitement and depression of the central nervous system and eventually convulsions and death.

Calilla - A joint. *Cigarro de marihuana, filtro*.

Cocaina - Cocaine.

Guilla'o - A marijuana high, to be stoned, baked.

Kenke - *Marihuana, ganja, mota*, weed, pot reefer, joint.

Marihuana - Marijuana.

Panama Red - A cultivar of *cannabis sativa,* with a high level of THC, named for its bud's clay-like red color. **Possession of marijuana is illegal in Panama.** But you already knew that.

Papeleta - *Basuco* cigarette-rolled in paper. A dose contains a mere 0.5 grams of cocaine.

Pichi - Cocaine. *Dícese comúnmente a la droga cocaina*.

Piedra - Rock. Crack cocaine. Literally stone, rock or ice.

Piedrero - A homeless person whom is hopelessly addicted to crack cocaine.

Porras - A joint.

Quémao - Toasted. Stoned on weed. Same as *Tostao*.

Quén Qué - *Marihuana*.

Tostao/a - Someone who is high on weed. *Thomas/Manuelita tostao de tanto fuma.*

Verbs - Los Verbos

A

Aguaitar - To spy, to watch stealthily.

Apachurrar - To intimidate, to bully. *Apabullar.*

Arrancar - To party. To go to a party *Salir de fiesta.*

Arrancarse - Literally, to pull off, to tear off. To get drunk. *Emborracharse.*

Arranquear - To go out, to party and get drunk.

Arropar - To make love with your clothes on. *Hacer el amor con la ropa, comünmente visto en saraos o en lugares con poca intimidad.*

Aweitar - To wait, or to spy on.

B

Bicicletar - To go somewhere. I'm going.

Birrear - To play. *Jugar. Birriar* We were *birriando* football all afternoon.

Blazear - To offend. Can used as a gerund. Rosa is bothering me. *Rosa me estaba blazeando. Ofender.*

C

Cabrear - To bother, harass. *Molestar.* One of the must common verbs in Panama, used when someone is getting tired of doing something or when someone is becoming bothersome. To be fed up with. *Estoy cabreado* - I'm tired of this. *Me tienes cabreado.* I'm fed up with you.

Chachariar - To complain. *A ella si le gusta chachariar.* She likes to complain.

Charcotear - To take a short cut. *Cortar camino.*

Chequear - Check or review, to monitor. *Revisar, controlar. Esta semana no he chequeado mi correspondencia.*

Chifear - To ignore a person. To avoid. *¿Estas me chifeando?* Are you avoiding me? *Chifea ese awebao porque es un loser* Don't invite that guy because he is a loser.

Chifiar - To trick someone, or to be tricked by someone. To prank.

Chiliar - To chill. *Vamos a chiliar en el chantin.* Let's go chill at the crib.

Chinguear - To bet. *Apostar.*

Chopear - To shop.

Chotear - To greet.

Chupar - Literally, to suck. To drink alcohol. *Ingerir bebidas alcoholicas, libar alcohol.*

Conguiar - To scam or to fleece, especially to cheat a Gringo victim. ¡*No te dejes congiar!* Don't be taken for a fool!

Cortarse totuma - To get one's hair cut

Cranear - To think hard. To give thought to.

Culear - Vulgar way of saying to have sex.

D

Dale valor - To give value to. To amplify. To turn up the volume on a sound system. *Fren, dale valor a esa plena.* Friend, turn up the music.

E

Echar un cinco – 1. To take five, to take a break, to sleep for a little while. Panamanians don't take siesta, they take five. *El panameño no toma siestas: Echa un cinco.* 2. To fight.

Enchilorar - To arrest, detain, arrest.

Enchuchar - Drunk. *Enchucha engomado, con resaca ensaltar. Enhebrar.*

Engomado - Hungover. *Con resaca.*

Espatillar - Spread the knees. *Abrir las piernas.*

Ensaltar - Inebriated. *Enhebrar.*

Estar bravo - To be angry.

Estar en fuego - To be drunk.

Estar pelao - To be without money. To be broke.

F

Friquear - To bother. To freak. From the word freak in English.

Fugarse - To skip class. *No dar una materia en la secundaria.*

G

Gorrear - To bum drinks. *Tomar tragos a costilla de los demas.*

Gruvear - To get busy with someone, as in a one night stand. Also, to goof around with them. Allegedly the verb originated when former Republica de Panama, President Mireya Moscoso, cheated on Arnulfo Arias with a man named Gruber. People gossiped that Mireya was *grubeando.* Eventually she and Gruber were married and she became Mireya Moscoso de Gruber. An alternative explanation is that *gruvear* is derived from the English word Groove as in we're grooving.

Gruviar - To bother or annoy someone.

Guevear - To lose track of time. *Perder el tiempo.*

H

Hanguear - To hang out.

Huevear - To egg around. Like a hen sitting on its the eggs in its nest. Not doing anything productive. Today we aren't going to do a thing. Comes from *awebao*. Also a synonym of hanging out. (see *Parkear*).

I

Irse al kinder - To make a mistake.

J

Jumarse - Commonly used instead of *emborracharse* (to get drunk).

L

Libor - *Tomar bebida alcoholico*

M

Marear - *No me vengas a estar mareando.*

Machetzo – To strike a powerful blow with a machete, as in slashing prices. Also, yhe name of a department store in Panama, Panama.

Mulear - To plod, to trudge. *Caminar. Engañar para no pagar una deuda o favor.*

N

Nada que ver - Nothing worth seeing. To be worthless.

Nachar - To rob.

P

Pa - Short for para (for), as in *esto es pa' ti.* (this is for you).

Pajar - To masturbate. *Volar cometa.*

Palanquear - To use one's influence to help another person get a job or to score with member of the opposite sex.

Parkear - To hang out, or to park your car.

Pariciar - To party.

Paviarse - To skip school. *Faltar a la escuela.*

Pelar el bollo - To hit the ball, to die.

Petatearse - To die.

Pifiar - To show off. To boast. *Presumir. Quiero pifiarte mi moto nuevo.*

Pilar - To study. *Estudiar, estudiar con afón pilón(a) es alguien muy estudiso o sabelotodo.*

Ponchar - To fornicate. *Fornicar. Panmanians don't make love, they ponchan. El panameño no hacen el amor, sino que ponchan.*

Puyarse - To pinch or to wound with a sharp object. *Pincharse o herirse con un objeto punzante.*

Q

Quémar - To burn. To be unfaithful. To betray. To cheat in a relationship. To burn a bridge.

R

Rajarse - To put on a splendid party or other activity. *Mostrarse espléndido u obsequioso al ofrecer una fiesta o cualquier otra actividad.*

Recabuchar - To lust, to desire, to crave; to have an obsessive sexual desire. *Lujuriar.*

Refinar - To eat.

Repellar - To eat, even though you may have just finished eating.

Reventar, detonar, romper - To tease or to mock another person.

Rofear - To incite or start a fight.

S

Sacar la chucha - 1. To beat up 2. To be involved in a really bad accident. *Sacale la chucha a ese man* Beat up that guy up. *El camioneta se saco la chucha.* The truck got wrecked.

Sacarse la - To fall. *Caerse*

Sacarse la mierda - To give a hard smack. *Darse un buen golpe.*

Sae - Shortened form of the Spanish verb *saber* (To know).

Sainear - What a poser does. To pose, or to put on a false appearance or false impression.

Serruchar el piso - Literally sawing the floor. To discredit someone, to pull the rug out from under them.

Shifear - To jilt, to avoid. *Dejar plantado, evitar. Vamos a shifear a Rodolfo para que no vaya a la fiesta. Mis compañeros de clase me hicieron un shifeo.*

Shotear - A shout out, a greating. *Saludar.*

Sopear - To sweat. *Sudar por las axilas y hacer marca en las vestimenta.*

T

Ta - Short for *Está (is)*, as in *Ta bueno*. It's good.

Tavuel - *Vuelta* Reversed. To go out. Sometimes pronounced *Tawer*. *Vamos a dar una tavuel.*

Tener concha - To have balls, to be daring, adventurous. *Ser osado, atrevido. ¿Que te pusiste mi ropa? ¡Sí que tienes concha!*

Tener mococoa - To be lazy or bored. *Tener pereza o estar aburrido.*

Tira lirica - Convince, persuade. *Convencer.*

Tirar la bomba de humo - To throw the smoke bomb. To distract attention away form something. *Irse de algun lugar sin que nadie se de cuenta.*

Tirar la mano - To fight. *Pelear.*

Tirar los perros - Haircut. *Cortejar..*

Togarse - Dressed well, elegantly. *Vestirse muy finamente.*

Tomar el pelo - To pull one's leg.

Transar - To swindle. To rob. *Estafar. El panameño no roba: Transa.*

Tripear - To enjoy. Derived from the English slang Trippin'.

V

Venirse - To come. A Panamanian doesn't ejaculate, he comes. *El panameño no eyacula: Se Viene.*

Vidajenear - To snoop. Poke into the lives of others. *Interesarse, hurgar en la vida ajena.*

Figures of Speech

A

A balazo - Rapidly. As fast as a speeding bullet. *Hazlo a Balazo.* - Do it quickly. *El panameño no va rápido: Va a balazo.*

A otro nivel - To the next level. *Mucho mejor que lo usual.*

Agarrar los mangos bajitos - To take the low mangos, which is to say, to take the easy way. *Hacer algo de la forma más facil.*

Agarrar una chiva - Literally, to grab a goat. To take a bus.

¡Ajo! - Garlic, literally. But in slang it's an exclamation expression of surprise or amazement.

Al detal - *Venta al detalle o al por menor.*

Ala orden - You are welcome. At your service.

¡Alla! (*¡Ayala!* and sometimes pronounced 'áshala') - An exclamation of surprise or anger derived from *Vaya la.*

¡Alla la bestia! - Holy Cow!

¡Alla la maquina! - Another expression of surprise.

¡Alla la ñex! - Expression that denotes surprise or amusement. Very similar to Holy Shit!

¡Alla la vida! - An expression of surprise, like OMG when something bad happens.

¡Alla la vida! ¡Chuleta! - Used to politely replace the offensive word *mierda*, which means shit.

Alla onde uno - From the television show *Hecho en Panama,* it means hometown. *¿Tu eres de alla onde uno?*

Anda con la awebazón al hombro - Moving really slowly. Or taking a long time to think about something before getting around to actually doing it.

¡Ay Papa! An expression of excitement. *¡Ay Papa!, vamos pa a visitar Iowa!*

A lo loco - A crazy, haphazard way.

Arranque (de arrancarse [irse de fiesta/a parrandear]) - To go to a party. *Parranda.*

Arrebatiña, pata y puñete - What happens after hitting the *piñata*. *Lo que pasa despues que alguien rompe la piñata.*

Arroz con mango. - Rice with mango. A bad, bad situation difficult to resolve. *Encontrarse en una situación dificil de solucionar.*

Awebao - As in, *Si awe, no awe.* Idiot. Idiotic.

B

Baja panty - Strong liquor. *Bebida alcoholica.*

Bajarse del bus - The head of or in charge of. *Patrocinio de alguna cosa.*

Blazeando - She is bothering, and or, annoying me. *Ella me esta blazeando.*

Boca de picha - A foul mouth.

Bolitas de quiñar - Marbles. *Canicas.*

Botaste - La botaste - Means that you did something awesome. Comes from the English baseball figure of speech. To hit it out of the ballpark.

Buco rantan pocoton - A lot of something. *Cantidad.*

C

Cara de nalga - Face like an ass.

Casa de la verga - Place far away. *Lugar lejano.*

Casa del rayo - Obscure location. *Lugar escondido de la faz de la tierra.*

Chapaleo de ahogado - Moving forward knowing the course is dangerous. *Acción de seguir esforzandose por conseguir algo sabiendo que la causa está perdida.*

Chicha e paipa - Watered down. *Agua.*

Chicha 'e Piña - Literally means pineapple juice, but in Panamanian slang it means easy or unimportant. As easy as pie/*piña.*

Chicha de policia - Water. A policeman's drink. Agua.

Chiqui show - Drunken spectacle. *Espectaculo bochornoso.*

Chilearte - Chill, buddy.

Chivo loco - Play dumb. Pretend not to notice. *El que se hace el desentendido.*

Chor chuchon - Shorts. *Pantaloncito.*

Chucha- frickin - A popular expression used in phrases like: *Chucha madre.* ¡Sombitch! (sic) *Este chucha vaina-* This frickin thing. Not considered blue language.

Chucha de tu madre - Son of a whore. *Hijo de mama, prostitute.*

Chucha madre - *Insulto.*

Chuleta - Literally a porkchop, except in Panama where it's an expression of anger during road rage, or when you are incredulous at an exorbitant price. ¡*Chuleta loco! (Pero, chuleta es un diminutivo de chucha que en Panamá es una palabrota).* ¡*Que problema*!

¡Chuso! - Darn it! Non vulgar way of saying *chucha*. Like saying fudge instead of the F- word.

Coje turumbo - Get out of here! ¡*Vete de aqui!*

Cojelo suave - Chill out. ¡*Cálmate!*

Colmo - The last straw.

Coma sea - Any old, expedient, improvised way. Jury- rigged.

Come arroz - Rice eater. A little boy. *Hijo.*

Come bollo - Eat pussy. A saying common in la Chorrera province. *Dicese del oriundo de la población de la chorrera.*

Comer en paila - To talk too much. *Hablar excesivamente*.

Comiste en paila - A chatter box. Someone who is always talking.

Como ñingaño - But of course. Yes.

Con el huevo encima - Slow moving as if carrying eggs. ¡*Miralo! Anda con el huevo encima!* Look at him! He is so slow.

Con la papa en la boca - Literally, with a potato in his mouth. Someone talking in a pompous manner. Think Mr. Howell from the 60's-era TV show Gilligan's Island.

Corbata de gatito - Cat tail. Bow tie. *Corbata de lazo.*

!Cuando no? - But of course!

D

¡Dale alante! - This can mean one of two things: Either hurry it up, or go away! The context will give you a clue. *Dale pa' tras* - Go all the way to the back of the bus.

Dale cuero - Literally, give it leather, as in horse reins. Do it fast.

Dale pues - Go for it.

Dar pena - Panamanians say *Me da pena* when something is embarrassing or bad. *Ese cantante da pena. Canta muy mal* (He's embarrassing he sings so badly).

De alante - From the front, the top, meaning something that is awesome, great or cool.

De aqui a la China - Literally, from here to China.

Déjame una perdida al cel - When you call, just let it ring once. *Cuando te llamen a tu celular, dejen que suene una sola vez.*

De la high class - Describes someone who is high class or is acting high class in an uncivil manner. Often said sarcastically as in: *Con la papa en la boca, Hay si, ella es de la high.* Yeah, she's high class. *El se cree de la high.* He thinks he's high class.

De repente - All of a sudden. Slang expression meaning: Possibly. It could happen. Used in context: *De repente, salimos por alli.* - Possibly, we'll go out there tonight.

Despues dicen qué es uno - They don't practice what they preach.

Dime el bochinche - Tell me the uproar, the latest gossip.

E

El de las pelotas - Of the balls, see *juego vivo*.

El que quiere azul celeste que le cueste. - To get something good you have to fight for it. *Alcanzar algo necesita un esfuerzo.*

Ella es un pie - She is beautiful.

En Belen con los pastores - Literally to be in Bethlehem out with the sheperds. Absent minded, lost in thought.

En panga - Literally to be out on a boat. Un- cool, un- interesting, un- hip. *Tas en panga.* You are a dork.

Escuchalo plena - Listen to the full. To pay attention to.

Eso no es - That isn't. Something is not right at all.

Está bien pretty - Something nice.

Está en la podrida - Literally rotten, decomposed. *Estar mal.*

Está hablando paja - He's talking straw, telling lies, saying stupid things.

Está limpio - Literally to be clean, to be broke.

Están velando - Watching someone eat, which is impolite.

Estas ne la papa - To hold a good position in government employ. *Bien colocado en un puesto del gobierno.*

Estoy Harto - I'm fed up. Super full of food.

Estoy Salado - Literally, I am salty. I have bad luck, I am unlucky.

¡Esto es una ñameria! - This is foolishness!

H

Habia buqou de gials en la ponchera - There were a lot of girls at the party. *Buqou* is of course from the French *beaucoup*.

Hasta la requete - Drunk.

Hasta la tuza - Up to...

Hasta la verga - Extremely drunk.

Hay que tener la palanca - To have influence. *Tener influencia.*

Hice una cagada - Literally, I made a shit. I made a mistake.

Hiquillo se porta como un chiquillo - He acts like a little kid.

I

Ir a pelarse - To go get a haircut. *Ir a cortarse el cabello.*

Ir por fuera - To get out. I'm outta here. *Rosa ya va por fuera. Acompáñalo a la puerta.*

Ir a tocar el arpa - To go to play the angel's harp, to die.

J

Jo pirigallo - To express grief, sadness. *Expresa dolor o susto.*

Juego Viva - Literally, to play alive. Which means to take advantage of a situation. To go for it in an unfair way.

L

La botaste - Meaning that you did something awesome, great or cool Similar to the English phrase: You hit it out of the park.

La hace - It does it, meaning something cool or awesome.

La ultima coca cola del desierto - Literally, the last coca-cola in the desert. Something valuable. In *yerga*, meaning, when someone is the best of the best, at the peak of their game.

Lecho grado S - Ejaculate, semen. *Lecho conyugal.*

Listo para la photo - Literally, ready for the picture, (Hollywood reference to the classic movie Sunset Boulevard starring William Holden) but in Panama it means to be so wasted you or they can barely function. During carnivale in Panama, Panama you encounter lots of revelers who are *listo para la photo*.

Lo chekea - Check it out.

¡Los Locos Somos Mas! - Literally, There are more of us crazy people! A slogan popularized by the Ricardo Martinelli 2009 Presidential Campaign after the opposing party's candidate Balbina Herrera called Martinelli *loco* (crazy).

M

Me lo paso por los huevos - I just don't care. See *Me sabe a cake*.

¡Me quemo! - Literally, she burned me. She cheated on me.

Me sabe a cake - It tastes like cake to me, meaning, I don't give a damn.

Me vale verga/un pepino/un comino - It doesn't matter to me.

Me viene con tiempos a mi - Which is to say acting violently. *Quiere decir que la persona actúa de una forma en particular o violenta contra otra.*

¡Meto! Man! Hey! - General exclamation used for any number of things, an expression customary of people from the Panamanian province of Chiriqu. *¡Meto! Man! Meto! Qué te pasa* - Man! What's wrong with you?

Mi Amor - Honey - Hun - My love - Obviously used when speaking with a loved one, or with someone you are comfortable with, or being friendly with. A woman cashier might playfully call a male customer, *Mi Amor,* when quoting the price of merchandise. Men and women also use this term when flirting. *¿Mi amor, como te llamas?* What's your name, Love?

¡Miercoles! - Wednesday, the day of the week. Slang usage similar to Man used in exclamation.

Mi nave - Literally my boat. Meaning my car, my ride.

N

Ni chica ni limonada - Neither juice nor lemonades. Which is to say, not one thing or the other.

¡No me jodas! - Stop bothering me. Literally, don't fuck with me.

No me parece - Expression of discontent. *Frase popularmente utilizada para demostrar descontento por algo.* I don't think so...

¡No frieges! - You're joking! Exclamation used when a person doesn't believe something. *¡No frieges! Se casaron de verdad?* You're joking! They're really married?

No hombre - No way! Exclamation used when a person doesn't believe something or for emphasis. ¡*No hombre!*

¡No'ombe que va! - No. *Proveniente de No hombre, que va! No, nunca.*

No hagas eso - No way! Don't do that.

No seas maleducado - Don't be ill-mannered, poorly educated.

No tiene pepitas en la lengua - He doesn't have seeds in his mouth, he is unafraid to tell the truth.

O

Ofi and Oficial. - Yeah. Is it true? You betcha. Okay. Official. An exclamation that confirms agreement with what someone has just said. *Ofi, nos vemos el martes*.

Oiste - Literally, did you hear me? To confirm that you know what I am saying.

O Sea - A way to expressing surprise, disgust commonly used by *yeyes*.

Oye eso - Would you listen to that . . .

P

Pa dio - I don't know where it is. *No se donde esta.*

Pa la bajada - To the finish. *Al final.*

Pai pai y no estoy - Panamanian boxing technique made famous by former world champ Jaime Rios. Punching your opponent then taking a step back.

Palabra sucia - Dirty word. *Palabrota.*

¡Pálante! - Forward! Go for it! *¡Para adelante!* shortened. But in slang means leaving or abandoning a party or place. *Fui palante.* I left.

Pelar el bollo - To die. Literally, to peel the tamale.

Palato pa' ti - The discounted price you pay at the Chinese store (Inexpensive).

Pan de pueblo - Anybody's woman. Bread of the whole town. *Mujer cualquiera.*

Parche pegao - *Novio(a) inseparable.*

Pasa un cuara - Gimme a quarter.

Pelan - *¡Pálante!* shortened.

Por fuera - To leave.

Por fuerait - Means out, I'm gone. I'm outta here!

Puesto quémao - Literally, that place is burned. That seat is already taken, by me!

Puro Tilin Tilin Y Nada De Paleta - All bells and no popsicles, describes someone who says he is going to do something, but never follows through. All smoke and mirrors. *Tilin* is the sound of the ringing of the ice cream man's bell as he passes through the neighborhood.

Qué

Qué boba es ella - What a fool she is. Whatta moron.

¿Qué chucha te pasa? - Used when very angry, What the fuck is wrong with you?

¿Qué Cosa- Huh? - What the heck did you just say? More stylish than just what.

¿Qué le pasa a ese tipo? - Hey, What's wrong with that guy?

¿Qué lo que? - What's up? When texting, KLK. *Que es lo que pasando.*

Qué lunón, ó Qué Lunota - Sunny skies and no clouds. *Cuando hace mucho sol y sin nubes se ve redondo el sol al igual que la luna llena.*

¿Qué paso, loco? - What's up, man?

Qué vaina - What thing. WTF!

¿Qué Xopa? - What's up! *Xopa* spelled with an X instead of an S in order to avoid confusion with the word *Sopa* (soup).

Quiubo - The contraction of Que hubo. *Contratación familiar de ¡Qué hubo!*

S

Sacar la chucha - 1. To beat up 2. To be involved in a really bad accident. *Sacale la chucha a ese man* Beat up that guy up. *El camioneta se saco la chucha.* The truck got wrecked.

Sacarse la mierda - To give a hard smack. *Darse un buen golpe.*

Salií el fulo - The sun just came out.

Se agotaron - They ran out of something, as in out- of- stock merchandise.

Se dejo congiar - She was taken for a fool *(congo).*

¡Se estrampo la vida! - She hurt herself!

¡Se la llevo! - She or he won the prize money. She won it all. He took it.

Se le aguaron los helados - They watered down the ice cream. A coward. *Cobarde.*

Se le moja la canoa - His canoe is getting wet or sinking, refers to a man acting effeminate.

Serruchar el piso - Literally sawing the floor. To discredit someone, to pull the rug out from under them.

T

Ta - Short for *Está* (is), as in *ta bueno* (it's good)

'Tá bien - It's good. *Estábien se le da significado segün la dicción, pronunciación y el tono de la voz usada por la persona Algo sorprendente falso.*

Ta bueno - It's good.

Ta cruel - *(estí cruel).* When something is really bad, or really good.

Tá gallo - Uncool.

¡Ta mundial! - It's world Class!

¡Ta pifioso! - It's neat!.

¡Ta rareza! - Means it's rare, but denotes coolness.

Tas' Ahorcando Al Padre - Literally, you are choking the priest. You have a wedgie.

Tas en Bosnia - Not in the moment. Lacking situational awareness.

¡Tas loco! - You are crazy. Like the English WTF!

Tas pescandoa - Person who is going to go out and pick up someone of the opposite sex/sexual. Literally, going fishing.

Te estoy reventado - Literally, I am blowing you up. I'm making fun of you.

¡Te Explico! - Lemme tell ya, buddy!

Tengo goma - Literally, I have gum. I am hungover.

Te dehaste ganar. - Ooh! You let him win!

Te quiero cojer - I want to fuck you.

Tirar cinta - Literally, to throw the tape, to tell a story.

To cul - It's all good. It's cool.

Tomando el pelo - Joking. Yanking my/his or her chain. Pulling his leg. Joking.

Tomárselo suave - Take it easy.

Tomate con manga larga - Literally, take yourself a long sleeve. Drink a large beer.

Trepa que sube - A very bad situation.

Tu no eres la guial de la foto - Literally, you are not the girl in the foto. *No te conozco de ningun lado.*

V

Vale cebo - A saying that describes un unjust or stupid situation *Situación injusta o estúpida.*

Vama de los perros - Clean. *Limpio.*

Vamos a hacer una vaca - Literally, let's do a cow. Let's take up a collection (of money).

Vigilando la tienda - To vigilantly watch the store.

Volar la cometa - To masturbate. *Masturbarse.*

Vamos pal cuero - Go for it. Let's get to it, let's do it. To take action. To perform any non particular action.

Vamos pal war - Let's have sex. Literally, Let's go to the war.

¡Vamos de arranque! - Let's party.

Voy a agarrar los mangos bajitos - I will find an easier solution.

Voy a mimi - Baby talk for I'm going to sleep now.

W

Wappin - Wappin you - What's happening. A friendly greeting similar to *Xopa*.

Dictionary – Diccionario

A

Abanico - Literally a fan. Colloquially meaning to fan out one's cards. To show one's cards. *Extender las cartas en abanico. Ventilador en cualquiera de sus presentaciones.*

Abdulia - - Ugly woman. *Mujer fea.*

Abuelazón - Doting grandparents spoiling their grandchildren.

Agarrado - Muscle guy, meat- head.

Agarra'o - Buff. Someone with well developed muscles, like a soccer player's legs. *Persona de musculos desarrollados.*

Agua cero - Torrential tropical rain.

Aguaita - To wait. *Esperar.*

Aguaitar - To spy, to watch stealthily.

A guanchinche - Mounted on a horse, piggyback. *A caballito, cargando a espaldas.*

Agrandao - Arrogant, conceited. *Presumido.*

Aguevado - Clueless. *Sinónimo de guevon o aguevoniado.*

Ahuevado (*normalmente dice ahueva'o*) - Stupid. An insult. *¿Estas ahuevado?* Are you stupid? *Sinónimo de huevón, lento, imbécil, idiota.*

Ahuevazón - Stupid situation caused by an idiot. *Situacion calificada de ahuevada.* Situación causada pur una tontera/por un tonto.

Alazon - A streak of bad luck, an unfortunate event.

Alegrabarrio - A woman prone to starting loud fights in the middle of a *barrio* (neighbourhood.)

Alelao - An idiot. Variant of *awevao*.

Allala (aveces pronunciado también áshala) - Expression of surprise or anger. *Interjección de sorpresa o enojo. Adaptado de Vaya la, usualmente utilizado con palabras curiosas y soeces. Ayala peste, áyala máquina, áyala vida.*

Allá adonde uno - The interior regions of Panama. *El interior de Panama. Pronunciado: alla 'onde uno.*

?Alla la peste! - To express anger or surprise. *Interjeccion de enojo, sorpresa, etc. ?All? la peste!? No encuentro su pasaporte!*

¡Allala vida! - A Panamanian expression with numerous variations like: *¡Ayala bestia!* among other phrases where *ayala* is followed by off color, or vulgar words.

Amigososa - - Best friend. *Gran amiga.*

A monchinche - Mounted on a horse, piggyback. *A caballito, cargando a espaldas.*

Apachurrar - To intimidate, to bully. *Apabullar.*

Apagon - What happens when the IRHE cuts electric power (outages).

Arrabalero/a - Troublemaker. *Buscapleitos.*

Arraiján - A western city and district/province of Panama. The origin of this nameplace is in dispute. Competing between the plant *arrayán* and the English abbreviation for at right hand and the name of an indigenous chief. *Distrito al oeste de la provincia de Panamá; aunque su origen se disputa con el de la planta arrayán abreviación del inglés at right hand o del nombre de un cacique famosa de nombre parecido.*

Arranque - Literally, the starting point but as slang means party *Vamos pal ₀ Arranqué! Let's go to the party! Fiesta en la noche. El*

Arranque. One for the road. As in: *Esto es el arranque.* - This is the last one I'm gonna have.

Arranque (de arrancarse [irse de fiesta/a parrandear) - To go to a party. *Parranda.*

Arrebatiña, pata y puñete - What happens after hitting the piñata. *Lo que pasa despues que alguien rompe la piñata.*

Arrecho/a - A sexually excited, horny person. *Persona que esta excitada sexualmente. Persona que puede realizar cualquier trabajo o hazaña (termino utilizado con mayor frecuencia en el interior del país.*

Arrepinchoso/a - Someone who likes to party. *Persona que le gusta el arranque.*

Arropar - To make love with your clothes on. *Hacer el amor con la ropa, comünmente visto en saraos o en lugares con poca intimidad.*

Arroz con mango/Trepa que sube/pandemonio - Literally, rice with mango. A tough situation. *Grandes problemas.*

Arrancarse - To get drunk. *Emborracharse. Me arranque con unos amigos que no vea en mucho tiempo.*

Atolladero - Out of the way. *Area de dificil acceso.*

Auto - The common car. *Automóvil.*

Awebao - An idiot. *Una idiota.*

Awebasonor Ahuevason - Things that are foolish or just plain dumb. *Awebao* is derived from the root word *ahuevado* (egg-headed). Depending on the tone of voice it can be either derogatory as in idiot, or friendly as in dude. Pronunciation varies: *awebado, awebao,* or *aoaooo.*

Azuero - The peninsula in the Central Provinces that includes Herrera, Los Santos and part of Cocle and Veraguas.

B

Babylon - The police.

Backeo - Back it up, back it up.

Bad Buay - Bad boy.

Bagre - A particularly ugly woman. *Mujer horrible o poco agraciada físicamente.*

Bajareque - A misty rainfall in the highlands. Think cold and overcast. *Llovizna menuda y persistente a partir de diciembre, extendiéndose hasta febrero. Durante este período los días son sombríos y fríos.*

Balboa – 1. A unit of money in Panama. One Balboa equals one U.S. dollar. Also know that la República de Panama circulates US greenback dollars, although the country mints its own coins whose value is interchangeable with US coins. Know that instead of the dollar sign $, the Balboa is represented by the letter B, for Balboa. 2. The brand name of a Panamanian beer.

Baño de pueblo - Participating in a folkloric event celebrating Panamanian culture and food. *Participar de alguna actividad normalmente de tipo folklorica para renovar el espiritu Panameno. Irse a un pindin, cantaderas, comer frituras, baile tipico.*

Barra - A group of people, fans. Similar to groupie in English. *Grupo de personas que apoyan a un solo participante de algun concurso o competencia.*

Barriada bruja o barrio brujo - A ghetto. A miserable place. *Villa mísera o Favela.*

Bascula - Pawn shop. Literally a weight scale, which is the universal symbol for a pawn shop.

Bate - 1. An exageration. An excuse that's hard to believe. A whopper, an outrageous lie. *Exageración. Excusa difícil de creer, o golpe de suerte.* 2. A spliff. A big joint. *Un cigarro de Marihuana de gran tamaño.*

Batería - A cheat sheet. Paper with the answers to a test. *Papel con respuestas de un examen.*

Batida - Police operation. *Operativo policia.*

Batsai - Buttocks. *Trasero en la mujer or hombre.*

Bellaco - Skillful. Clever. *Habilidozo.*

Bemba - Swollen lower lip. *Labio inferior abultado.*

Bergington - Derived from *berga* which means penis but in slanguage it means Holy shit! or an expression made when somebody is amazed or excited. This comes from the television program *Doble vida* (double life). Normally said ₀*Ayala bergington!.*

Beri beri - Also see *Faracho*. Derived from epilepsy attacks.

Berraco - Noisy brat. *Persona diestra, hábil, furioso, dificil.*

Berrinche - Stink. A disagreeable odor. The strong odor of urine. *Fuerte olor a orine.* This bathroom stinks of piss. *Este baño huele berrinche.*

Bezaca - The head. *Cabeza.* reversed.

BFM - Poorly dressed. Acronym for *Bien Foking Mal. Se usa cuando una persona esta mal vestida.*

Biencuidao/Biencuida'o - Person who hangs out in parking lots near shopping centers, movie theaters, churches and watches cars while people do their business. It's wise to pay protection money to them in advance or you risk returning to find damage to your car: ie A keyed door, scratches), flat tires. When motorists return to their cars, he will ask for a tip saying, *bien cuidao*, reminding you that he looked after the car in your absence. *Persona que cuida carros. Individuo que se gana la vida cuidando autos y consiguiendo estacionamientos en lugares como centros comerciales, discotecas, cines, almacenes.*

Blotin - Brother. G*ringuerismo, hermano.*

Birecua - Something that is not as it appears. A line that appears straight but isn't. *Linea que parece recta pero no lo esta*

Birria - A team game. A video game. *Juego ya sea de un deporte de equipos o de consolas de video juegos. Juego muy repetitivo sin espiritu de competencia o finalidad alguna, comunmente usado para los videojuegos, futbol o baloncesto.*

Birrial - To play a friendly sport or game 2. To be hooked in some kind of activity. *Vamos a echar una birria de beisbol. Juan tiene una birria de jugar Nintendo. Qué no se la quita nadie).* Also used as a verb, *Estoy birriando esa cancion.*

Birrioso - Someone obsessed with some thing. *Persona que tiene una aficcion exagerada por algo.*

Blanco - Cigarette. *Cigarrillo. El panameño no dice cigarrillos. Dice Blancos.*

Blin Blin - Bling, jewelry.

Blod - From blood. Brother of the blood. A close friend. *Hermano de sangre. Amigo muy cercano.*

Bobo - Fool. *Tonto.*

Bocacha - An ugly woman. *Mujer fea.*

Bocarest - Bad breath.

Bochinche - Gossip. *Chisme.*

Bochon - *Chombo* reversed (black guy).

Bofetada - A slap in the face (cheeks). *Cachetazo.*

Boleta - A traffic ticket, a civil citation.

Bomba - Gas station. *Estación surtidora de gas.*

Bongo - Native canoe.

Boquiflojo - Gossipy. *Chismoso.*

Borrador - Eraser. A Diablo Rojo or a big truck, usually roaring down on you. As in it will wipe you out. Eraser. See Diablo Rojo. *Un gran Autobüs o Camion.*

Borriguero - 1. A small reptile from the lizard family. *Reptil pequeño de la familia de los lagartos, muy ágil y asustadizo.* 2. A low-ranking employee. At a construction site it is the *borriguero* who does the hard work. *Trabajador de baja categoria.*

Botarla - Lazy. *Decir alguna atorrancia.*

Botarate - A reckless, spendthrift. *Hombre atolondrado y derrochador.*

Bote - Hitch a ride. *Pedir que te lleven o te den un aventon a algun lugar.*

Botella - Bottle. *Persona que recibe sueldo sin trabajar.* A useless employee hired because of connections (see palanca), rather than qualifications or willingness to a work. *Persona que cobra pero no trabaja.*

Bravos de Boston - The Boston Braves, referring to the 1914 World Series of baseball champions: Meaning the best of the best. *El mejor de una profesión. Dedicado a los bravos de boston de 1914.*

Buchí - Corruption of the English bush man. A rather unsophisticated fellow. *Corrupción del inglés bush man: hombre silvestre, sin cultivo.*

Brother surfer - What surfers call each other.

Brujo - Cheap. Of poor quality. *Barato. De poca calidad.*

Brutal - Phenomenal. *Fenomenal.*

Brutongo - An ignorant brute. *Super ignorante o bruto.*

Buay - A guy, a man. Colon English/Congo Spanish. *Chico, muchacho.*

Buco - A lot, a great deal. *Mucho o muchisimo. Bastante.* Fom the French *Beaucoup. Galicismo derivado de beaucoup.*

Buche - Belly. *Barriga,*

Buenon - Handsome. *Guapo.*

Bueno/a - Fine. Hot. Used to informally describe a sexually appealing person. *Guapo. Ese mujer esta bueno!* That woman is fine *Que esta muy bonita o bonita y tiene buen fisico. Como en es un pay.*

Bufeo - Dolphin *Delfin.*

Bulto - Somebody you don't want around since they give you nothing but trouble. *Persona que no tiene un buen desempeño de sus funciones, viene de ocupar un espacio determinado siendo irrelevante para la situacion.*

Burundanga - Junk food. *Alimento de poco valor nutritivo, como: Caramelos, chocolates, et cetera.* 2. Sweet. Unhealthy. *Dulce. Comida chatarra, no saludable.*

C

Caballada - Nonsense, drivel. A ridiculaous act or saying. *Burrada, hecho o expresión disparatados.*

Cabreado - Boring. *Aburrido.*

Cabreatee - To leave alone. *No molestes.*

Cabriao - To bother or molest. *Aburrido.* Tired of something. *Arto.*

Cacharpa - A rickety, old car. *Automóvil viejo y destartalado. Tiene una cacharpa que casi no puede andar.*

Cachetón – Chubby cheeks. *De cachetes o carrillos abultados.*

Cachimba - A pipe. *Pipa de fumar*

Cachimbín - A know- it- all. From the Brazilian word *Cachimba*, - A smoking pipe.

Cacique – 1. An Indian chief during colonial and postcolonial times. 2. A local political boss in Spain or Latin America. Eg Cacique Comagre.

Cachucha - Beret. *Gorra.*

Cafí - A hard slap in the face (lash) or the side of the head (*coscorrín*). *Una Palmada fuerte átras en la cabeza.*

Cagada - Shit.

Cagalitroso - Old man. Also, *Cagalitroso* junior (around 50 yrs old) or cagalitroso senior (older than 70)

Calilla - Marijuana joint. *Cigarro de marihuana.*

Camarón – 1. Day work performed by a handy man. From the English: Come around... *Trabajo temporal de jornada corta.* 2. To earn extra money. *Matar un tigre o hacer alguna cosa para ganar dinero extra.*

Camaroncito - Casual labor. A day worker. During the US occupation of the canal, when Panamanians were looking for work, Americans responded, "Come around, come around." *¿Voy a conseguir unos camaroncitos por ah? pa' comprar algo de comer.*

Cangreja - Ugly woman. *Mujer fea. Mujer de baja categoria que usalmente sale por las noches y no puede caminar normalmente de tanta profesion. Baja la marea y suben las cangrejas, un expresion que se usa cuando cae la noche en Panama.* Land crabs that come out at night.

Canillas - Legs. *Piernas*

Cañon - Yucca and ground beef. *Compuesto de yuca y carne molida carrizos pajilla. Seguro sucederá.*

Carajal - In quantity. *Gran cantidad.*

Carajo! - Damn! (Only marginally stronger).

Carimañola - Panamanian/Colombian meat-pie shaped in a torpedo-shaped yuca fritter, stuffed with cheese, seasoned ground meat or shredded chicken and fried.

Carrizo - Skinny like a reed. Literally, a drinking straw. *Pitillo, así que ya saben, aquí nada de mandar al carrizo a nadie porque de verdad no lo entenderían.*

Carro - Car. *Automóvil.*

Cartucho - The ubiquitous plastic bag. *Bolsas en general.*

Casa bruja - Very poor house, a shanty made out of wood scraps and/or zinc built on squatted property. Literally a Witch's house.

Casa del culo - A place located in the middle of nowhere. Literally House of the ass.

Cayuco - A canoe- like vessel carved from a tree trunk and used by indigenous Panamanians.

Cegato - A nearly blind man, someone who can barely see and wears *Lentes de culo de bottella.*

Centavo - Centísimo.

Chambon - Incapable or incompetent.

Cinta - Story. Gossip. *Hey, te tengo una cinta!* Hey, I have a story! *Cocoa and bochinche.* Literally, a tape.

Cizaña - From the *cizaña,* a nuisance plant. In *jerga* it means to grow discord; to cause strife between persons. Used with the verb *meter*, as in *meter cizaña/sizaña*. Or, *sembrar cizaña (sizaña).* To sow discord, to talk gossip, or even to lie in order to cause discord. *¡Eres un sizañoso!* You're a trouble maker!

Cizanero/mete candela - A troublemaker, someone who makes trouble, instigates a fight.

Click - In Panama, the sound you hear at the end of a telephone conversation. No goodbyes or any other formality, just the sound of hanging up.

Coblan - *Blanco* reversed.

Cocho - Smack alongside the side of the head with the knuckles. *Golpe en la cabeza propinado con los nudillos de la mano. ejemplo Te* *voy a dar un cocho!*

Cocoa - Like a war story, the recounting of an event. *Chisme Cuento o historia relacionada a un suceso o evento, normalmente un 'bochinche' o chisme.*

Cocobolo - Someone who is either bald or losing their hair. *Calvo.* Also, hard wood from a tree used to make local handicrafts.

Cocobola - An angry woman. *Mujer fea.*

Cocorrón - Smack on the side of the head with the knuckles. *Golpe en la cabeza propinado con los nudillos de la mano.*

Cocotudo - Someone with money. *Persona adinerada.*

Cof - Cuff. Smack to the head. Golpe que se dá en la cabeza con los nudillos de la mano

Coima - Money received for no work. *Recibir dinero por no poner una multa.*

Cojenalga - *Problema.*

Colmo (el colmo) - The last straw.

Colon Buay - A Colon dude.

Comearroz - Child or baby. A rice eater.

Cómico - Someone unimportant, a joke of a person. *Juan es un cómico, no sirve para nada.*

Comisariato - Commisary for economy priced food. *Economato.*

Comiste en pailaa - Chatter box, chatty Kathy, a person who talks too much.

Compa - Amigo. *Frase cariñosa refiriendose a un campesino o a un compadre... buen amigo.*

Con colon - Rice stuck to the bottom of the pan. *El arroz que queda pegado a la paila.*

Conflei - Corn Flakes. *Se pronuncia Conflei. Hojuelas de maíz, todos*

los cereales son conflei. *Cualquier cereal de cualquier marca que se come en el desayuno, del inglés Corn Flakes.*

Congo - A rube, a sucker, someone gullible, easy to deceive. Also the African culture from Colon province.

Conguear - Rob. Embezzle. *Estafar.*

Cool (se pronuncia cul) - *Bien, bueno, tranquilo.*

Cool - A good thing. *Algo bueno o chevere. Tranquilo*

Copa - The airline of Panama, which is affiliated with Continental Airlines.

Corozos - Corrupt politicians. *Pezones corrupto, politicos panameños.*

Coscorrón (normalmente *cocorrón*) - *Insecto redondo y cafe, golpe dado con los nudillos (vease cocho.)*

Cranear - To study. *Estudiar.*

Cromar - Fellatio. Polish the chrome. *Felacionar. La felación, una práctica de sexo oral.*

Cuara - From the English word quarter. *Originario de la palabra quarter - 25 centavos moneda de 25 centavos.*

Cuatrera - Literally a rustler. A woman on the prowl. A prostitute. *Mujer la cual esta en busca o acecho de algun hombre cazado.*

Cuatro gatos - Very few people. Literally, four cats.

Cucurucho - A tiny, ugly house or place.

Cueco - An effeminate man, homosexual. *Hombre afeminado, homosexual man o lesbiana.*

Culantro - A beautiful woman. *Una bella dama. Proveniente del Segmento Doble Vida del programa televisivo Parecen Noticias. Tambien es una un planta que se utiliza para sazonar la sopa y otros alimentos.*

Culear - Vulgar way of saying to have sex. *Manera vulgar de decir tener relaciones sexuales o sexo con una persona.*

Culei - Bebida Instantánea Kool- Aid. Refresco de frutas artificial pulverizado.

Culia - Sexo.

Culicagao - Literally ass- shitted. A moron or cowardly person. A very young person: laopecillo, pelaito.

Culillo - Terrible, soul- gripping fear. *Miedo.*

Culitripi - Powerless. Skinny person, ugly and weak. *Sin fuerza.*

Culito - Ver Pay

Culo - The butt.

Culo de Botella - Bottom of the bottle (coke bottles). Refers to eyeglasses with extra thick lenses.

Curda - A drunk. *Borrachera.*

Curso - Diarrhea.

Cus cus - Tough, short, wirey hair. Nappy.

Cus Cushard - Short, nappy hair.

Cuscu - Wild, unruly hair. *Cabello tieso o rebellde.*

CH

Cha - Used to give emphasis to your words. *Se usa normalmente al decir cualquier frase para hacer enfasis de algo). Ejemplo (cha fren vas a llegar mañana a la party)*

Chacaleria - Folks from the ghetto.

Chacalate - Dirty water. *Agua sucia. Chocolate.*

Chacara - A countryman's bag; commonly used for balls (testicles).

Chacaron(a) - Superlative for *Chacara* means a very lazy man (or woman) or, someone who relies on everybody else to solve their problems.

Chacarudo - See *Chacaron*.

Chachai - Baby clothes. *Vestido de niña.*

Chaineado - From the English Shiny or shined up. Dressed up *bien vestido Chaneado (originario de la palabra 'shining persona que esta bien vestida.* Chakalito (chakal, chacalito) - Ghetto youth. Often used in a pejorative way to describe an individual with gold teeth who listens to reggae or reggaeton, and wears gangsta clothing topped off with punk hairstyling. Thug lifestyle.

Chalchicha - Sausage. *Salchicha.*

Chamai - Yellow cloth to wipe and dry a car. A chamois.

Chambín - A clumsy person *Que demuestra mucha torpeza al hacer alguna labor o trabajo. Torpeincapaz.*

Chance - Chance. Opportunity, possibility. 1. *Oportunidad, posibilidad.* 2. A two- digit lottery ticket.

Chaneao - Well dressed. *Bien vestido. Tallao.*

Chantin - From the English, Shanty. Home, house. A humble abode. A Panamanian doesn't have a house, he has a *Chantin. El panameño jamas ha tenido una casa: Siempre ha tenido su Chantin'.* Vamos pa' mi chantin - Let's go to my house. *Yegate a mi chantin.* A humble abode.

Chapot - From the English Shaped- up. Someone very well dressed. *Estas bien chapot. Bien vestido.*

Char cot - A short cut.

Charcotear - To take a short cut. *Cortar camino.*

Chata - Someone with a skinny ass.

Chécheres - Worthless objects. *Objetos sin valor. ¿Porque traes la* *bolsa siempre llena de chécheres?*

Chen- chen - Money. *Dinero.* From Mandarin chinese *Chien*, which has the same meaning.

Chequear - Check or review, monitor. *Revisar, controlar. Esta semana no he chequeado mi correspondencia.*

Chevere - Cool. *¡Qué Chevere!* How cool.

Chicachille - *Calle en geringonza chi.*

Chicachisa - House. *Casa.*

Chicha - A fermented beverage. *Refresco o bebida fermentada. Léase cualquier tipo de bebida en polvo que venga en bolsitas tipo Tang, et cetera.*

Chichi - *Bebé. Forma cariñosa de decir Bebe. Forma cariñosa de deicirle a novia o novio.*

Chichína - A bump on the head or swelling elsewhere on the body.

Chifear - To ignore, to shun. *Ignorar. No invitar/ignorar a alguna persona.*

Chilin - To chill, as in relax. *Del ingles. Chilling estar tranquilo parkear cool estaba parkeando chillin en la chantin.*

Chimbilín - Money. *Dinero. En esta familia siempre hace falta chimbilín.*

Chinchorro - Bow tie. *Corbata de lazo.*

Chingongo - Chewing gum. *Goma de mascár(chicles).*

Chingia - Game. *Juego.*

Chinguear - To bet. *Apostar.*

Chino o Chinito - The Chinaman. A small grocery store. Kiosk. A corner store. Back in the 1800s many Chinese migrated to Panama to help build the Panama Railroad and so it should come as no big surprise to learn their descendants today own many corner stores. Hence, the name. *Bodega. Tienda de abarrotes dícese porque generalmente están. Tienda de abarrotes atendidas por asiaticos.*

Chiquishow - Putting on a show. A fistfight spectacular. *Dicese de un espectáculo pügil no programado en el que los combatientes por lo general no saben pelear de forma vistosa. También utilizado para indicar cuando a alguien le hacen un espectaculo frente a otras personas, regularmente realizado por el sexo femenino.*

Chirola - Jail *Cárcel.*

Chirrisco - Homebrew booze made from corn or sugar cane. *Bebida hecha en casa proveniente comünmente de la fermentacion y destilacion del maiz o la caña.*

Chispa - Literally, the word means spark, used as a verb it means to be very sharp. *El esta bien chispa*. He is sharp.

Chitre - Sand flea.

Chiva - Literally means female goat, but also means small bus. Not to be mistaken for *una diablo rojo. Me voy en chiva pa' Chitre*. Transporte colectivo de capacidad media. Obsolete mass transit bus (converted schoolbus)*Autobüs de transporte colectivo.*

Chiwiz - A snack. *Orignario de la palabra chesse wiz. Una merienda.*

Choborro (a) - Brusque person. *Persona brusca y de poca capacidad para desarrollar una actividad.*

Chocao - Drug addict. *Drogado.*

Cholipay - An attractive *mestiza* or Indian woman. *Cholita y pay. Una mujer mestiza/indígena atractiva físicamente*

Cholito - A not so nice way of referring to Kuna Indians. Also used to refer to someone as being ignorant, a country bumpkin.

Cholo - Rural person. In the interior it refers to a friend, in the city a person from the interior. So, a city slicker versus an amigo. *Persona rüstica, de pueblo pequeño, o que se comporta como pueblerino. En zonas del interior haciendo referencia a amigo, en la ciudad hace referencia a personas del interior.*

Cholometal - A mestizo or indigenous person (Read: brown skin), who dresses and acts the part of a rock and roller. *'Cholo' o indigena que sigue modismos de roqueros, punks y/o heavymetals.*

Cholopop - A cholo wannabe. Person from the countryside, trying to impress by wearing rocker outfits. *n 'compa' que acaba de llegar a la capital vestido como en los 70s', con el pecho afuero y usando essencia de pacholi como perfume.*

Cholywood - *Forma graciosa, despectiva o una manera para definir la farándula panameña.*

Chombo - African word for a black man. Many people find this word pejorative. *Persona de piel muy oscura Nuestros llamados afrodescendientes persona de raza negra.*

Chonta - Head. *Cabeza.*

Chori - Countryman, buddy. *Paysito.*

Chorrerano - Someone from Chorrera provicne. *Dícese del oriundo de la población de la chorrera.*

Chota - *Minivan de la policía. También utilizada para referirse a joder.* Derogatory term for a large police car, pickup truck or van used to transport detainees from demonstrations, protests or curfews.

Chotear - Friendly greeting. *Saludar Dícese de un saludo amistoso que puede o no ir asociado a golpearse las palmas de las manos efusivamente en señal de celebración o aprobación. En las regiones del interior del país la connotación puede también estar ligada a embromar (vacilar) a otro, mediante un chiste o una broma.*

Chuain - *(de pronunciación rápida)* Well to do. *Esta es un sinónimo de Yeye y es una persona acomodada, alta alcurnia, delicada o adinerada.*

Chucha - Vagina. *Chucha. Coño.* Vulgar way of referring to the female reproductive organ. This word can be used in dozens of connotations. It can denote anger, happiness, surprise, sadness, speechlessness. *Chucha, Qué bien me fue! Chucha Qué mal me fue! Chucha no se como me fue! Estoy en chucao.* (I`m pissed). *Vulva* también usado como interjección. ₀ *Véase Congo. Te 'tan (están) cogiendo de congo! Someone who is alwaChucha!, Que chucha me importa!*

Chuchita - Someone who is always being taken advantage of by another.

Chuchon - A big pussy (person).

Chuleta - Spoken to express surprise. *Exclamacion de sorpresa o admiracioncuando algo esta mal interjección. !Chuleta, Fíjate por donde vas, que ya casi me pisabas!*

Chumbo blanco - A white nigger. Please don't use this offensive figure of speech.

Chuncho - Car, auto, truck. *Automóvil, coche, carro.*

Chupasangre - A high-maintenance woman, a blood sucker. *Mujere de alto mantenimiento.*

Chupata - *Una fiesta.*

Churria - Explosive diarhea. *Ganar con mucha ventaja.*

Churrusco - Same as *cus- cus*. Extremely curly hair.

Chutri - *Interjección.* Used to expresss a negative surprise.

Chuzo! - Non- vulgar way of saying *chucha* meaning, Darn it, et cetera. Like saying fudge instead of fuck. *Ver Chuleta.*

D

Daim - A dime, ten cents. *Moneda de 10 centavos.*

Dale - To be in agreement. *Estar de acuerdo.*

Dandy - A man who seduces many women. *Un hombre que seduce muchas mujeres.*

Dar bote - Bounce around an idea. *Que te lleven.*

Datien - Tienda reversed. *Traspalante de tienda.*

Deboka - Bad person. *Mala persona.*

De huevo a pelota - *Aprendez por que aprendez.*

Del otro comando - Homosexual.

De a vaina/De a vainilla/por un pelito/ por un cocoazo/por pura leche - *Ganar algo por pura buena suerte en el ultimo momento.*

De agencia - New, cool. *Nítido, bonito, nuevo.*

De alante - From the front/top. Something awesome, great or cool.

De kíoon - Unstoppable.

De leys - Something that is happening no matter what.

Demencia - Crazy, wild, demented. Awesome. *Qué demencia ese carro.*

Desguaíangao - Messed up, disheveled, badly dressed or beaten up.

De vez (en cuando) - Occasionally, now and again. *De una vez, en el acto de vez en cuando.*

Diablo rojo - Red Devil. Now obsolete, formerly brightly painted school buses formerly used for public transport. In March of 2013 these privately- owned means of public transportation were phased out, replaced by municipal transit Metro Buses. *Autobus generalmente pintado de varios colores procedente de las escuelas estadounidenses que comúnmente se les llama borradores por el efecto que produce durante una colision.*

Dola - *Un dolar.*

Doble cara - Two- faced, a hypocrite. *Eres manso doble cara.*

Dulce de leche - Flavorful, caramelized condensed milk.

Duro - Hard. Frozen fruit treats served in a plastic cup. *Refresco de frutas congelado en una bolsita plastic.*

E

Echar un fly - To go defecate. *Ir a defecar.*

Echar un polvo - To make love. *Hacer el amor.*

Echarse un cinco - To take a nap. *Tomar una siesta.*

Ediondo - Bad smell. *Huele mal.*

Embolillar - To fight. *Pelear.*

Embustero - A liar.

Emparedado - Sándwich.

Emparapetao - To fix something in a very slipshod manner. Jury-rigged. Usually with duct tape. *Tienes el bumper del carro todo emparapetao.*

Emm pe - Awkward moment, when someone tells a joke and nobody laughs. *Botate.*

Empollerada - A woman or girl wearing the national dress of Panama, *la Pollera.*

Emputarse - To bother. *Molestarse.*

Emputazón - To bother. *Molesto.*

Enante - A moment ago... *Hace un momento.*

Enchilorar - To arrest, to detain, to put in jail. *Arrestar, encarcelar, detener.*

Enchuchao - Angry. Upset. *Enojado, molesto. Carlos está enchuchao con Verónica porque ella no quiere salir con él.*

Enchuchar - Drunk. *Enchucha engomado, con resaca ensaltar. Enhebrar.*

Enfrascarse - To fist fight, to get into a fracas. *Pelear. Agarrarse a golpes con otro embolillarse.*

El de las pelotas - Of the balls. See *juega vivo.*

En Bosnia - Bosnia means you are nowhere to be found. In his own world. *Ese man esta en Bosnia..*

En panga - Un- cool, un- interesting, not at all hip. *Tas en panga* - You suck.

Enculado - Very in love, especially at the beginning of a relationship. *Felipe estí enculado.*

¿Entonces? - So, what's new? Or, what's up?

En tuco - Broke. No money. *Sinonimo quiebra de no tener dinero, hace referencia a cuando un automovil esta montado sobre pedazos de madera, generalmente sin llantas o en reparacion.*

En verga - Poor quality. *Algo de mala calidad, no complaciente al gusto de nadie ese show esta en verga.*

Eso ni es - When something is just not right. *Man, eso ni es.*

Equis - Literally the letter X, standing for the deadly poisonous Fer de Lance viper.

Espatillar - Spread the knees. *Abrir las piernas.*

F

Facafama - Bed in geringonza. *Cama en geringonza fa.*

Faityn - Street fight. *Pelea callegera.*

Falefache - Milk. *Leche en geringonza.*

Falto liquipeiper - Liquid paper. Mistake corrector. *Palabra usada para los correctores liquidos.*

Falta de todo - Completeley lacking in: Glamour, respect, elegance. *Significa falta de respeto, falta de ética, falta de elegancia, falta de clase, falta de consideración, falta de todo.*

Faracho - Heart attack. *Moridera que empieza con una calentura en el pecho que sube a la cabeza.*

Farachoataque - Heart attack. *Le dio un faracho!le dio un ataqué/colapso). Syn. beri- beri, jaratac.*

Farril - Derived from the English figure of speech for real, in Panamanian Jerga it means real fun.

Fashion - Stylish. In fashion. *Ella si esta fashion con ese vestido.* - She's really stylish in that dress.

Ficha - Cutting, stabbing weapon, knife. *Arma punzocortante.*

Firi- firi - Very skinny man or woman. *Ana es una firi- firi.* In superlative: *Bien firi- firi.* Extremely skinny!

Fitness - In shape, to be fit, in good physical condition. To describe someone that is in shape. *¡Ahora si estoy fitness!* Now I'm in good shape.

Flintin - A couple fighting, sparks flying, the woman throwing things. *Guari- Guari Patois, referente a una pareja peleando, donde la mujer le tira cosas 2. Flintin también tiene significado de creerse más de lo que es o molestar: es un flintoso, viene con mucho flintin.* Flintin also has the meaning of believe most of what is or disturbing, a flintoso, comes with much flintin.

Flojo - Coward or a lazy bones. *Cobarde o perezoso.*

Flus - Cash money. *Qué va, hoy voy a chupar en mi chantin porqué no tengo flus.*

Focop/focót - A fuck up. *Feo, en mal estado.*

Fregón/a - An annoying, bothersome person. *Persona que molesta, fastidia..*

Fren - Friend. Buddy. Dude. *¡Qué xopa, fren! Amigo.*

Fres - Slippery. Someone fresh or smart-alecky. *Tu eres lizo! ¿Porque me tocaste?* You are fresh! Why did you touch me?

Fresco - Without embarrassment. *Sin verguenza.*

Fría - Beer. *Cerveza. Pasame otra fría.*

Friqueo Freaked. Bothered. Concerned.

Friquear - To freak out. *Molestarse, Friqueado.* From the English freak or freak out. *Qué friqueo, no me quedó na' de moneda.*

Frulo - To be afraid of something. *Tener miedo.*

Fritanga - Food cooked with a copious, if not excessive, amount of oil. *Comida cocinada con exceso de aceite.*

Fugarse - To skip classes. *No dar una materia en la secundaria.*

Fula/o - Blond, blonde. *Rubio. Andrés está enamorado de una fula. Esa fula está buena!* That blonde is way hot!

Full explotá - Attractive woman. *Mujer muy buena.*

Fulo de farmacia - Dyed hair. *Cabello tenido con tinte.*

Fundillo - Anus. *Especificamente el orificio anal.*

Fuste - Rear, rear end, bum, back side, ass. *Nalgas, trasero.*

G

Gadaca - Transposed *cagada*, or shit. *Traspalante de cagada(algo que sale mal de momento).*

Galicismo - A word derived from the French language.

Gallina - Coward. *Cobarde.*

Gallinero - General admission. The cheap seats. *La entrada general o area popular de algun evento cultural (concierto) o evento deportivo.*

Gallo - Awful, distasteful, a cheap object. *Ese pelicula estaba bien gallo.* That movie sucked big time. *Barato, de poca calidad persona sin gracia. Artefaco de mala calidad y orginario.*

Galluza - Bangs, hair. *Flequillo de cabello sobre la frente.*

Gancho - A clothes hanger.

Gapin - Penis. *Pinga.*

Garnatí - A hard slap in the face.

Garnatón/Garnatada - A cuff or violent blow with the hand to the face. *Bofetón. Garnatada normalmente se dice garnatá.*

Garra - Friend. See *Fren*.

Gasopin - Quickly. *Rápido.*

Gatosolo - Literally a lone cat. The venerable raccoon, also *coatimundi.*

Geringonza - Dialect from the ghetto. *Dialecto revolucionario hablado por los jovenes.* See *Jeringonza*.

Ghett - Ghetto. *Calle o agrupacio libros debajo de su puesto y alguinos ni siquiera son tuyos.*

Gial - Means girl, but not a little girl, or *niña*. But instead, a term of endearment for women.

Globito/forrito - Condom. *Condon, preservativo forrito ha sido popularizado por el homónimo personaje condón del popular programa La Cáscara.*

Gogrin - Gringo reversed.

Golpe de ala - Body odor. *Olor que emana cuando no se usa odorantees.*

Goma - Hangover. *Resaca. Malestar fisico despues de una borrachera.* The physical discomfort you feel after binge drinking.

Gorrear - To bum drinks. *Tomar tragos a costilla de los demas.*

Gorrero - A moocher. Someone who lives off others. *Persona que le gusta livar a costilla de otro.*

Grajo - Body odor. Smelly armpits. *Apestoso. Olor que emana cuando no se usa desodorante hueles a grajo.*

Grajobad - Underarm smell. Stinky armpits. Body odor.

Gringo - An American. *Estadounidense.*

Grubeo/ar - Estar con una persona por un tiempo o por una noche para pasarla bien y para nada serio o formal.

Gruviar - To bother. *Molestar.*

Guabazo o Guabanazo - A hard punch. *Gran golpe, usualmente seguido de hematoma de alguna clase.*

Guachiman - Night watchman. Security. *Celador nocturno. Seguridad* Also see *wachiman. El panameño no es celador sino es Wachiman (watchman or security guard).*

Guacho - A soup. *Es una sopa espesa que lleva ñame, yuca, culantro, arroz, verduras y alguna carne, que puede ser res, rabito de puerco o chicharrón. El guacho se sirve tradicionalmente en una totuma, plato que se fabrica partiendo a la mitad unos frutos redondos y duros que crecen en el monte. Tambien siginfica la combinacion de varias cosas. Plato de arroz cocido con carne y verduras que parece sopa espesa.*

Guagua - A beat up wreck of a car. *Se dice de un automóvil muy viejo o en mal estado.*

¿Guapin/Juatapin? - A greeting: What happened? What is happening? *Saludo que indica que pasa. Del inglés.*

Guapote - Someone with low self-esteem. *Individuo usualmente con poca autoestima que hace mucha fisicultura pero que al final siempre sigue siendo bien feo.*

Guari- guari - An indigenous dialect, a mix of Spanish, French, English and local dialect. *Dialecto de la Provincia de Bocas del Toro, es una mezcla de Español, Francés, Inglés y lenguas indígenas.*

Guaro - Alcohol. *Bebiba alcohólica licor.*

Guevear - To lose track of time. *Perder el tiempo.*

Güey - Dude, Man. *Este Güey.* This man. Pronounced whey.

Gufi - Goofy. Nuts.

Guial - Young woman. Derived from the English word girl. *Mujer, chica, a*lso see *Gial*

Guichi guaiper - Windshield wipers. *Limpiaparabrisas.*

Guaricha - Kerosene Lamp. *Lampara de kerosene.*

Guilla'o - High on marijuana.

Guillado (normalmente se dice guilla'o) - 1. High on drugs. *Influenciado por alucinógenos 2. Emocionado, inspirado.* When someone tries to understand a concept, but becomes even more confused than when started.

Gulicripa - Literally speaking, a dance move. The term comes from the Jamaican slang *Gully Creepa,* which quite literally means a ghetto backstabber who embraces the thug life in order to hide from police and steals from his or her own friends.

H

Habla claro - To speak the truth. *Habla con la verdad.*

Hablar con los monstruos - Talk with the monsters. *Vomitar* See *Llamar a Hugo.*

Hablar paja - To make small talk. *Decir trivialidades, no decir nada importante.*

Hacer la cama - Literally to make the bed. To put aside differences or take what is utilimately yours. *Tratar de hacer a un lado a alguien o quitarle lo que le pertenece. Le vamos a hacer la cama a Miguel para* *quedarnos con su dinero.*

Haitiano - Genre of Haitian music. *Genero de musica del pais en mencion (que misteriosamente pocos saben el nombre) es que nisiquiera entendemos lo que cantan(esta en frances) y hasta inventamos el estilo de baile.*

Hard - Miserly, *Tacao.*

Harto - Full. *Estar lleno.*

Hasta la güacha o hasta las zapatillas - To be very, very drunk. *Que está muy ebrio(a).*

Hasta la verga!! - To get drunk. *Pasarse de tragos.*

Hasta la tuza - Generally used to express up to the point where drunk.

Hediondo - Stinky, smelly. *Que huele mal.*

Hijo de la Luna - Man from the moon ie, an albino Kuna Indian.

Hojaldre - Masa/flour frybread.

Hooooombeee... - Same as *Ayyyyyyyy..*

Horquilla - Clothes pin.

Huevear - To waste time. *Perder el tiempo de la peor forma.. Pónte a trabajá y deja de 'ta webiando!*

Huevín - Idiotic. *Idiota.*

I

Igueputa - Sonuvabitch. *Hijo de puta.*

Inchi pinchi - Inseparable friends. *Amigos que siempre están juntos.*

Interior - The interior of the country meaning the provinces.

Provincias.

Ir al choque - Go to the crash. To confront an issue head on. *Ir de frente ante cualquier adversidad.*

Is *(pronounced eess)* - Yes, reversed to *si. An* affirmation or simply, yes.

Istmeño - Isthmian, of the isthmus of Panama. A Panamanian. *Panameño..*

Istmo - The Republic of Panama, which coincidentally just happens to be an isthmus.

J

Jaquima - A horse muzzle. *Bosal utilizado para controlar caballos.*

Jartar - To eat. *Comer.*

Jarto - Full stomach. *Lleno de comida.*

Jefe - A Boss - How to address someone in charge of a situation, in higher authority, or at work. An acknowledgment of respect.

Jerigonza - See *jerga.*

Jerga - Slang, argot. Supposedly derived from *jerigonza* meaning a difficult language to understand. A special language of a trade, one used by those in the know. In Panama *jerigonza* means street slang. Mumbo jumbo, jibberish.

Jeta - Mouth. *Boca.*

¡Jo! - Denotes affirmation, surprise, exaggeration, admiration or anything that shocks, the meaning depends on the tone of voice. A shortened version of *¡Carajo!*

Joder - To bother. To joke with. *Bromear, molestar, irritar.* ₀*No me jodas!*

Joven - Miss or Mister. Often used to politely address a young lady working at a retail store or restaurant. Not normally used to address young men. Its usage avoids ambivalence with deciding between señora, a married woman, or señorita, an unmarried woman. *¿Joven, me puede dar la cuenta por favor?* Miss, may I please have the bill?

Juega vivo - To take advantage of a situation. *Con astucia, generalmente sin moral, oportunista.*

Jugo- e- Policia - Water. *Agua*

Julepe - Chaos. Confusion. *Caos, confusión, ajetreo. Tuvimos un julepe hoy en la oficina cuando vino un cliente a quejarse del mal servicio.*

Juma - A drunk. Pie- eyed. *Borrachera.*

Jumado - Inebriated. Drunk. *Ebrio.*

Jungla - The jungle. Panama's triple- canopy rain forest. *La Silva.*

K

Kacakasakado(a) - Married. *Casado o casada en geringonza ka.*

Kagukaakapo(a) - Good looking. *Guapo o guapa en geringonza ka.*

Kaikadikaokata - Idiot, an insult. *Insulto en geringonza.*

Karaojo – *Bueno.*

Keke - Cake.

La Kenton - When someone promises you something and then fails to deliver.

Ketona - Carton of cigarettes.

Kiosko - A small store. A kiosk.

L

Labia - Flattery. *Adulación, normalmente para convencer a la persona de cual es la mejor alternativa en una situación dada o para conseguir apoyo de la misma muy comun en el ambito de la politica.*

Láiter - From cigarette lighter. *Encendedor.*

Laja - Boulder. *Piedra enorme debajo o sobre un rio.*

Lambon - A sycophant. An ass kisser. *Persona que se vale de mentiras para obtener algün favor 2. Adulador.*

Lamparoso - *Lo que no que es.*

Laope - Boy. Pelao reversed. Also see *pelao*. *Muchacho.*

Laopecillo - From pelaito. Diminutive expression for little boy

Lavamí tico - Panamanian Laundromat.

Leche - To be lucky. *Tener suerte.*

Leche grado - Ejaculate. *Semén masculino*

Lechudo - A very lucky person. It also means milk. Variations are used as: What milk! *Lechudo: persona con mucha suerte. También se le dice lechero. En consecuencia, se utilizan ciertas variaciones como: ¡Qué leche! para decir, ¡Suerte!, mala leche, et cetera.*

Levante - Boyfriend or girlfriend who you like and there's chemistry between you. *Novio/a, quiénes se gustan y tienen química entre ellos.*

Licenciada - An easy woman. *Mujer de la vida fácil. Puta.*

Lickybuay - Young lad, *niño pequeño.*

Lif - A lift, a ride. *Aventón.*

Limado - Someone dead on their feet after a hard day's work or a drinking fest. *Dicese de la persona que se encuentra muy cansada luego de trabajar o beber mucho.*

Limpio - Penniless. Broke. Without money. *Sin dinero. Estar sin plata*

Lio - A problem. *Problema.*

Lisura - Smoothness. Daring. Bold. *Atrevimiento.*

Livar - To drink booze. *Tomar licor.*

Lizo - Smart-alecky.

Llamar a Hugo - To vomit. To talk to Hugo. To worship the great porcelain god. From the sound drunks make when vomiting.

Lleca - Calle reversed spelling. *Traspalante derivado de Calle.*

Llesca - Similarly, street. *Calle reversed.*

Loca - Gay.

Loco - A term of endearment for a close friend. *Es como se llaman los amigos de cariño. Muy comun entre oriundos de Panamá.*

Loco de porra - Mentally ill. *Enfermo mental.*

Loco man - Crazy man, but depending on context could simply mean man.

Lofu - *Fulo* reversed (blond).

Lomo - The back. *Espalada.*

Longtaim - A long time. *Hace mucho tiempo.*

Love lee verde - Hair straightener used by people with a very curly/afro.

Lyrica - Wristwatch.

M

Machín candao - To kick someone in the rear when he is bent over.

Machiua/Machigua/Machihua - See Cholopop. *Mas cholo que un Cholo Pop. Usualmente un indigena.*

Machoemonte - Tougher than Rambo. *Tipo mas tof que Rambo.*

Macua - A magic spell. *Hechizo.*

Made in Taiwan - *Persona de clase social.*

Mafá - 1. A food, *Abrebocas de harina (fritura) salado en forma de trenza dícese de un enredo, asunto complicado, o personas abrazadas de forma muy afectiva (como mafá).* 2. A complicated matter.

Maleante - Gangsta, a criminal. A *Racataca's* male partner. *Delincuente o persona que quiere ser como los delincuentes.*

Mami - A beautiful woman, or a woman who is outstanding at something. *Mujer guapa. ?Esa mami va a ser mía!*

Manacha Lesbian. *Lesbiana.*

Manacho - Young man from the working class with a good body. *Hombre joven de clase obrera, cuerpo atlético y aspecto un poco rudo y muy masculino.*

Man - Person. *Muchacho, hombre, pero se usa para referirse a cualquier persona, incluso mujeres (la man). También se usa de muletilla. Pero es que, man, no quiero ir man: muchacho, hombre Lorena anda con un man que es militar.*

Mandado - An errand.

Mandar a la verga - *Olvidarse de un asunto fastidioso.*

Manes - Youth. *Muchachos o chicos.*

Manso - Big or, really big. Immense. *Grande o muy grande.*

Mantelpiece de la buena - Butter, *mantequilla.*

Mantequilla de la mala - Margarine. *Margarina.*

Mantequilla de poca importancia - Irrelevant.

Manzanillos - Groupies. Fair weather friends. A rich or famous person's entourage that leeches off of them. So- called friends follow who take advantage. *Sin personalidad, influenciable con facilidad, también se dice así a los vividores.*

Marias - Maids.

Mariposa - A gay. *Hombre afeminado.*

Matapuerco o soplamoco - Literally, pork killer. A punch thrown without any technique. A hard smack that really hurts. *Golpe exagerado y certero, que duele mucho. Nótese que soplamoco es en la mejilla.*

Medias - Socks. *Calcetínes.*

Meía - See *Maleante.*

Memerre - Food. *Comida.*

Meñ - See *Maleante.*

Meña - Street youth. From the last four letters of *Panameña*. *Jóvenes de la calle de mal hablar y vestir. Denota las últimas 4 letras de la nacionalidad Panameña. También traspalante del tubérculo ñame),*

Meneito - Cheese chips or shaking/wiggling your butt (tail feather)

Menjurje - A concoction of disorder. *Mezcla desordenada de varias cosas..*

Meto - An expression of admiration. *Una frase de admiración y afirmación muy utilizada en la provincia de Chiriquí.*

Metoa - From Panama's Province of Chiriqui means someone has screwed up. See *Chuzo.*

Meximeños - *Mexicanos residentes viviendo en panama.*

Micha - Panamanian slang for vagina.

Micho - Cat

Microonda - Cockteaser. From microwave. They heat up but do not eat. *Calienta pero no come.*

Mili - Borrowed from military, to do something with disregard for authority, odds, or common sense. *Dale mili.* To go anyway.

Miliin - To dare. *Atreverse.*

Mococoa - 1. Lazy or bored. Drowsy. *Mococoase usa como sinónimo de pereza, aburrimiento, sobre todo si se acompaña de somnolencia.* especially if accompanied by somnolence. 2. Mucus. *Liquido producido por los miembros nasales, regularmente de color verde, esta se bebe en grandes cantidades usualmente luego de que a uno lo han traicionado (ver quemado) en una relacion se creia seria.*

Mogo - Dummy. Either a noun or adjective as an insult, but can also be used when kidding around. ¿Tu eres mogo? - Are you a dummy?

Mojón - Shit. *Mierda.*

Mol - A shopping mall.

Mola - In Dulegaya, the Kuna native language, the word *mola* means shirt or clothing. Traditionally, Molas are handmade using a reverse appliqué technique. But nowadays, many are machine sewn. Several layers (usually two to seven) of different- colored cloth (usually cotton) are sewn together. The design is then formed by cutting away parts of each layer. The quality of a mola is determined by such factors as: The number of layers; fineness of the stitching; evenness and width of cutouts; addition of details such as zigzag borders, lattice- work or embroidery; and the general artistic merit of the design and color combination.

Mommy - An attractive woman.

Monchis - Munchies in English. *Ganas de comer golosinas o otras comidas para picar. De la jerga en inglés munchies. Traje estos pistachos para bajar los monchis.*

Mongolo - Mongolian. An insult to denote stupidity, but can also be used when joking. *¡No seas mongolo!* Don't be a dummy!

Mongolizarse - Become moronic. *Volverse mongolico.*

Monstroseado - Really angry. *Enojado*

Montado(a) (normalmente se dice monta'o/a) - Portending healthy economics. *Que tiene buena situación económica*

Montonon - A huge quantity.

Montuno - The national folkloric attire of Panama worn by men.

Mopri - Cousin. *Primo trasplante.*

Mopri Cuz - Friend. *Primo* (cousin in Spanish) reversed. *Trato entre amigos. Ppersona que se cree con dinero. ¡Xopa, mopri?*

Moreno - It is more polite to call a black person *moreno* as *negro* can be offensive.

Motete - The bag a farmer's utilizes to transport products from the farm. *Bolsa de campesino.*

Mueca - To make facial gestures. *Hacer gestos con la cara.*

Mulea - To walk, to trudge. Plodding slowly like a mule. *Caminar.*

Mundeles - Belongings. Things. *Artículos indefinidos. ¡Y véte con todo y tus mundeles!* Get your shit and get out!

Muñequito puya puya - A Voodoo doll used in witchcraft. Popularized by Wanna Yuka Fruit (La Pepa TV).

N

Nachar - To rob. *Robar.*

Naitafón - Noche Alegre' (night of fun) - *Es una fiesta baililable nocturna con alegorias caribeñas que se celebra en una discoteca o* *generalmente en una casa donde hay muchas bebidas alcholicas y mucha comida, esencialmente de la comunidad afroantillana panameña.*

Natido - Fun. *Divertido, muy bueno. Dicen que la obra que vamos a ir a ver esta natida.*

Nave - Car. *Qué Nave Cheverre, fren.* Wow man, cool car!

Neto - Cool, awesome.

Nevera - Referigerator. Frigid. An air-conditioned bus. *Refrigeradora autobüs con aire acondicionado (dícese de los trans-provinciales Panamá- David frías). Mujer cuadrada.*

Ni chicha ni limonada - Neither juice nor lemonade. Which is to say, not one thing, or the other.

No Fitin - *No me pidan, no voy a brindar.*

No me parece - Expression used to express discontent. *Frase popularmente utilizada para demostrar descontento por algo.*

Nombe - Refusing to do something. *Negarse a hacer algo. Nombe mejor no vamos pa'alla.*

Nueve letras - Nine letters. Popular name for the highest selling brand of Seco in Panama, Herrerano, which coincidentally has nine letters.

Ñ

Ñame - Starchy root often used in soups. Also omeone crazy, *Loco.*

Ñamería - Craziness. *Locura.*

Ñampearse - Crazy. *Volverse loco/a.*

Ñampiao - Gone crazy, bonkers. *Gufi.*

Ñañara - Fear. *Miedo, terror o tremor a una cosa.*

Ñañeco - Someone behaving badly. *Persona que es malcriada.*

Ñángara - Disrespectful term for a Communist party member. *Forma despectiva de definir a los comunistas o miembros de partido de izquierda.*

Ñango - Backside. Butt. Ass. *Fundillo.*

Ñangotado/a (Añingotado/a) - Crestfallen.

Ñapa - Just a little bit more than you are already getting. Traditionally a little candle or some candies, from the early days of Panama and bought in Chinese stores. *Un regalo que dan cuando se compra algo en un tienda o abarroterria (introducido por los chinos para captar clientes frecuentes.*

Ñecks - Socially acceptable way to say shit. *Versión decente de mierda. Te wa (voy a) sacá la ñecks!*

Ñinga - Shit. Excrement. *Excremento.*

Ñáñara - Fear. Anxiety. *Miedo, terror o temor a una cosa.*

Ñítidocool - Awesome.

Ñorro - Gay man. *Hombre homosexual.*

O

Oh fasho - Okay.

Ofii - Okay, comes from oficial. To be in agreement. Use instead of *Esta bien o Es cierto..*

On - The word, no, reversed, meaning a negation or simply, no.

Oseaa - An abbreviation for *Lo Qué sea.* - Whatever. To express surprise or disgust. Popular usage among *yeyes*.

Otoe - A flowering plant eaten in soups as a replacement for potatoes. Synonyms: Taro, ñame, dasheen, malanga.

P

Pa - Short for *para* (for), as in *Esto es pa' ti.* This is for you.

Paciero(s) - A friend. *Amigo, generalmente amigos con quienes se comparte parrandas.*

Pa'lante - *Para adelante* shortened. *Reducción derivada de para adelante.*

Pai pai y no estoy - Panamanian boxing technique made famous by former world champ Jaime Rios. It consists of hitting your oponent and then stepping back.

Paja / Volar Cometa - Masturbarse.

Pajizo/a - A Jackoff. *Persona que se masturba constantemente persona que muestra debilidad ante una actividad física. Jo! no puedes ni levantar eso... 'tas pajizo!*

Pajear - A jackoff. Someone who masturbates frequently. *Masturbar pajiso. Persona que se masturba con mucha frecuencia.*

Paka - Contraband cargo of a drug dealer. *Cargamento de droga persona que tiene fardos/mochilas/ bultos [del inglés packs] referente a cartuchos de balas delincuente.*

Palabra sucia - A dirty word. Foul language.

Palanca - Bus driver. *Chofer del bus.*

Palante - The union of the two words *para y adelante* (literally: go forward) but actually means leaving or abandoning a party or place. *Fui palante* I left.

Palo - 1. A common word for a tree. 2. One Balboa. *Unidad monetaria de Panamá (Balboa). Acuérdate que me debes 10 palos.*

Pamper - Diapers.

Paloone - A dollar, also used for a tree.

Pana - A friend. *¿Pana, me das permiso?* - Excuse me, friend. (use when trying to squeeze by someone in a crowd. Also A good friend, as in *¡K sopa, Pana!* - What's up, man!

Panagringo – A US/Panamanian dual citizen.

Panahoochie - A Panamanian.

Panamá - Riches. *Ricos.* The land of abundant fish and butterflies. *Abundacia de peces y mariposas.*

Panama, Panama – Panama City.

Pankeke - Pancake.

Paniquio - State of panic! *Cuando una persona entra en estado de panico.*

Papi - Handsome man. *Hombre guapo. ¿Quién es ese papi que llegó con tu hermana?*

Paracaídas - Literally a parachutist, figuratively, a party crasher. *Persona que acude a una reunión o fiesta sin invitación.*

¡Parada! - Stop! A bus stop. Shout *Parada* to tell the bus driver you want to get off a bus.

Parapapeo - A carnival dance. The term is derived from the sound trumpets make. *El baile de las reinas de carnaval. Está parapapeando. El término se deriva del sonido de las trompetas de una murga: Para pa pá..."*

Parkin' - A party amongst friends. *Fiesta o reunión entre amigos.*

Parquearr' - To hang out. *Reunirse, Salir con alguien a pasar el rato: parquear con mis amigos poner a alguien en su sitio Quiso insultarme y lo parqueé. Normalmente la gente dice parquiar.*

Parrampán - A flamboyant costume. *Disfraz extravagante y ridículo utilizado en las fiestas de corpus cristi.* A pretentious person.

Pasar píramo - To be in dire straits.

Pasieero - A buddy.

Patacón - Plantain slices smashed and fried to a crisp. *Popular acompañamiento de comida, el cual consiste en rodajas de plátano aplastadas y luego fritas.*

Pataconcito - Little bit of trash. *Pequeña acumulación de basura, viene del relleno sanitario de la ciudad de Panamá (Cerro Patacón).*

Pataon - A good, hard kick.

Patatüs - Heart attack. *Desmayo, ataque cardíaco.*

Pati- amarillo - Cigarette with either a yellow or orange filter. *Cigarrillo con el filtro de color amarillo o anaranjado.*

Pato / ñorro / ñaño - Gay. *Ser sacalodo, tutifruti, punky- punch.* which is to say homosexual.

Patriota - Banana.

Paviarse - To skip school. *Faltar a la escuela.*

Pavo - Literally means turkey. Bus driver's helper on on Panamanian buses. He shouts out the bus route, the main stops and available seats. Also called a \Secretario.

Pay - Good looking person. *Hombre o mujer guapo(a) (originario de la palabra pie que significa dulce). Chica/mujer hermosso.*

Payaso/a - Arrogant. Stuck- up. Picky. A clown. *No seas payaso!*

Payola - Bribe. *Soborno a los dj.*

Pebre - Food. *Comida. Vamos a meterle duro al pebre en este restaurante.*

Pecipeupedad - City. *Ciudad en geringonza.*

Pecueca - Foot odor. *Mal olor en los pie,*

Pega- pega - Seeds. *Semillas de hierba que se pegan en los pantalones cuando se camina entre la malez comünmente en las peleas* *de gallos para cuantificar las apuestas.*

Pela - Any woman or chick.

Pela - A beating, mostly sports- related. *Los Bravos le dieron una pela a los Yankees.*

Pelaito - A youth. The diminutive form of *Pelao. Joven. Niño(a). Pelao. Muchacho.*

Pelao - Adolescente. A boy. Young man or kid. *Yo conosco ese pelao.* I know that dude. *Pelado: (sust.) niño, muchacho. ¿Dónde dejaste a los pelaos? / Esa pelada ya necesita cortarse el pelo. Lo trae siempre en la cara.* Derived from pelado (peeled). Refers to bald or hairless on pubes.

Pelo pelo - An exotic/erotic dance. *Baile erótico.*

Pelonera - Young boys game where the loser gets hit in the head. To playfully slap someone in the back of the head. *Golpiza propiciada entre varios sin ser fuerte, comünmente en la cebeza y en la secundaria.*

Pelucón - Man with long hair. *Hombre con el cabello muy largo*

Pendejo - Fool. *Tonto.*

Peon - Cargo. *Cargo de menor importancia en el trabajo del campo.*

Pepero - Pauper. A penniless person who collects soda and beer cans for their deposit. *Persona que no tiene nada y recoge latas.*

Perdida - A missed cell phone call, used to avoid burning up minutes. *Dejame una perdida cuando llegas.* Literally, Drop me a missed call when you get there.

Perigó - Needing a hair cut, *Necesidad de corte de cabello.*

Perro - 1. An unflattering opinion of a woman, a dog. *Despectivo utilizado como sinónimo de mujeriego usado como insulto.* 2. A player with lots of girlfriends upon whom he often cheats.

Perrón - Unpopular person. *Persona que no desempeña bien una funcion referenciada o exageracion de perro.*

Pescuezona - A big bottle of beer. *Cerveza de botella tamaño grande.*

Peso - A one- half Balboa coin. A half dollar. *Moneda de 50 centavos, viene del periodo de la separación de Panama de Colombia donde equivalía el peso colombiano a 50 centavos de dólar usado.*

Picando - Something in fashion or style. *Algo que está de moda.(Su uso se debe al famoso baile del pique, en Panamá.)*

Pichazo - A large quantity. A lot. *Un pichazo de gente.* (A lot of people).

Pichicuma - Someone selfish who doesn't like sharing food or money.

Pichi - Cocaine. Drug user. *1. Droga, dícese comünmente a la cocaina 2. Cocaína piedrero indigente.*

Piedra - Crack *(droga).*

Piedrero/a - Drug addict. *Persona drogadicta que ha llegado a la indigencia por ser drogadicto. Pepenador.*

Pifa o Pixbae - The fruit of a palm tree with the texture of a potato and a savory flavor of a smoked yam. When ripe it is a beautiful red fruit, when immature it is yellowish to green. With nearly the nutritional value of an egg , it is high in protein and contains beta- carotene, phosphorus, Vitamin A, some B and C, calcium and iron. Delicious when cook it is best when dressed in salt and honey. Called *chontaduro* in other Latin American countries it is reputed to be a natural aphrodisiac.

Pifia - Word used in the 80's to describe something cool.

Pifiar - To show off. To boast. *Presumir. Quiero pifiarte mis auto nuevo.*

Pifion - Vain. *Presumido.*

Pifioso - Admirable, impressive. *Impresionante.*

Pilar - To study. *Estudiar, estudiar con afón pilón(a) es alguien muy estudiso o sabelotodo.*

Pilinki - A cheapskate. *Persona tacaña*. Someone mean or petty. *Persona mezquina*.

Pilla - From the verb to look. *Mirar, Observar, atrapar. Pilla esto*. Look at this. *Te pillé* means I Gotcha.

Pillar - Synonym of to take. *Synonimo de tomar/coger/agarrar. Pilla la pluma*.

Pillí - Gotcha!

Piloto - A magic market.

Pingazo - Punch, collision, impact. *Trompon*.

Pingon - Big penis *Pene muy grande*.

Pinta - Cold, frosty beer. *Cerveza fría*

Piñatero - A baseball reference, when a batter swings at high pitch and misses he is a *Piñatero,* as in struggling to hit a *Piñata*.

Pipa - A coconut while in its youngest stage. Pipa water is a natural, refreshing drink.

Pincho - Meat on a stick, skewered. *Carne en palito*.

Pinga - Vulgar use of the word penis. *Bulgarmente pene*.

Pipí - Penis. Rigid member. *Pene, miembro viril*. A Panamanian doesn't have a *pene*, but instead has a pinga or pipi. *El panameño no tiene pene: Tiene pinga, pipí*.

Pipí sweet - A womanizer, a Don Juan. Literally, Sweet dick.

Piquete - Compliment. *Complemento o adorno a una idea*.

Pirigallo - Clitoris. *Femenino piropia*.

Piropiadera - A compliment. A dedication. *Cumplido*.

Pitufo - Small pickup truck or small, 2- door sedan, it literally means 'smurf' (from the popular TV show) but can also mean police trucks equipped with water canons that shoot a powerful stream of high pressure water onto rioters.

En pinga - Un- cool. Uninteresting, not hip. *Tas en pinga* (You suck).

Pixbae - See *Chontaduro*.

Plaga, plagatox - Rabble.

Plata - Literally silver. Money. *Dinero.*

Plena - Panamanian *reggaeton. Reggaeton* came from Panamanian *plena. Dj pon plena* (Dj play some plena.) *Reggeaton musica pegada Usado para canciones/ritmos de reggae pero también usada para otros géneros cuando la cancion es buena.*

Pluma - A ballpoint pen. *Boligrafo para escribir.*

Pocotón - Much. *Muchos.*

Pokemon - Someone ugly. *persona fea (hombre o mujer).*

Policia muerto - Speed bump. Literally, Dead policeman.

Pollera - The National Costume of Panama worn during festivals or celebrations and handmade of cotton and wool, predominantly white, but decorated with colorful flower designs *Panameñas* typically own two *polleras* during a lifetime: One before the age 16 and the other at adulthood. A *pollera* can cost from several hundred to several thousands of dollars and take up to a year to sew. The gold and pearl *mosquetas* and *tembleques* that make up a *pollera* are generally passed down as heirlooms through the generations.

Pollito - A handsome man. *Hombre guapo.*

Pollo - Girlfriend. *Novio.*

Ponchar - To fornicate. *Fornicar.*

Ponchera - Literally a bowl for serving punch but in Panamanian slang *ponchera* means wild fun. Also *ponchera* can mean something unusually cool, or scandalous. *Diversiòn. Hoy se formo tremenda ponchera en la discoteca.* Insanity. Madness. *Locura. Desorden, algarabía.*

Porcambín - Quite literally, pork and beans.

Porcón/millo - Popcorn. *Entiéndase popcon o palomitas de mais.*

Praka praka - A variation on the theme of *Rakataca*. *Derivacion de Rakataca.*

Preña - A pregnant woman. *Mujer embarazada.*

Priti - Pretty. *Bonito.¿Quiero comprarme un vestido bien priti para salir con ir? Del inglés pretty (bonito), sinónimo de cool. Que algo esta cool o nitidopriti.*

Pritty Cool - Good. Derived from the English word pretty. *Ese carro esta bien pritty!* That's a cool car!

Puesto quemado - A seat that is already taken. *Puesto reservado.*

Puñete - Punch with a closed fist. *Golpe con la mano cerrada.*

Pupu - Poo- poo. Shit. *Mierda y cagar.*

Push - See *Pushboton.*

Pushboton - A no- tell motel where you don't check in at a front desk, but instead, drive into private garage. Once inside, you pushed a button to close the garage door and gain access to a bedroom. *Un Hotel para tener sexo.*

Pusy - *Un Gay. Para decir homosexual.*

Puya - Machete with a sharp blade. *Un Collin. Machete largo y de punta aguda.*

Puyarse - To pinch or to wound with a sharp object. *Pincharse o herirse con un objeto punzante.*

Q

Quara - A quarter. *Moneda de 25 centesimos USD*

Qué bate - What an outrageous lie! Whopper of a lie. *Usado como* *descripció de algo ficticio, asombroso o espectacular.*

Qué bestia/Ayala bestia - What a beast.

¿Qué chucha te pasa? - Used when very angry with someone. Literally: What the cunt is wrong with you?

¡Qué huevo! - Literally, what eggs, means what balls! (*cojones*)

¿Que es lo que es? - What's up? Pronounced: *Que lo que é, o queloqué.Que hay de nuevo.* What's going on? Wanna piece of this? Sometimes used when defending someone and may be said right before a fight.

¿Qué sopa? - What's up? Greeting used among friends.. *Que paso* reversed. *Traspalante, derivado de ¿Qué paso?*

¿Qué sopa, loco? - Whassup, man?

Quén qué - Marihuana. Alternative spelling of *Kenke*.

¡Qué wecha la tuya! - That's rude!

Quebranto - Low grade fever. *Misteriosa elevación de la temperatura corporal no lo suficientemente alta como para ser considerada fiebre pero sí lo bastante seria como para faltar al trabajo o al colegio.*

Quema - A fire. To burn off of land in order to clear it for agriculture. *Incendio provocado de la maleza que cubre una parcela de tierra destinada a la agricultura.*

Quemar - 1. To be unfaithful in love. To cheat. To burn. *Ser infiel, engañar a la pareja. Cuentan que Braulio anda quemando a Silvia.* 2. To sell merchandise at a greatly reduced price. *Vender mercancías a precio muy reducido.*

Quemado/a - Cuckhold. *Persona a la cual su novio/novia esposo/esposa lo ha traicionado con otra/o.*

Quémao - Stoned on weed. Same as *Tostao*.

Quemaron - To be unfaithful. *Ser infiel.*

Quenque - Marijuana. Also see *Kenke*

Querosín - Kerosene. Petroleum- based fuel typically used in stoves and lanterns in the interior. *Petróleo que se usa para el alumbrado y para estufas.*

Queso - Literally, cheese. But in slang, means sexually attractive. *Cierta atracción meramente física y sexual.*

Quimbolitos - Cultivar of small and round beans. *Variedad de habas o judías, más pequeñas y redondas.*

Quincha - The *Quechua* (Inca) word for stone wall. In Panama, this borrowed word means a fence, wall, enclosure, corral, animal pen, constructed of wood, cane or giant reeds covered in mud and plaster. *Pared que consta de una armazón de parales atravesados por una serie de cañas transversales, recubierta de barro amasado con paja para darle consistencia.*

R

Rabel - Locally made violin used in folkloric festivals. *Violín de fabricación nativa empleada en la fiesta campesina de la mejorana.*

Rabi blanca - A dove with white tail feathers, also applied to the high social class. One fifth of Panamanians are Rabi Blancas, a Panamanian euphemism for the white butts/pale cheeks of the upper class. Term used to describe old money, a person of means. Literally translates to white- tailed. *Persona de plata. Paloma silvestre que tiene plumas blancas en la cola. Denominación aplicada a las gentes de clases sociales altas irónicamente*

Rabo - Dick. Literally, tail.

Rabodick - I'm going to cut your dick. *Te voy a cortar el rabo.*

Racataca / Rakataka / Rakaa - Someone from the ghetto. Originally it meant a *maleante.* A ruffian, a troublemaker, a ghetto recalcitrant.

Hombre o mujer sin clase, comunmente utiliza mayormente la jerga panameña autoctona (native). Derivado del sonido de las metralletas al disparar rakatakatakatakataka popularizado durante una canción del grupo Jam & Suppose en 1992: Over time the word *raka* has evolved to reflect pride in being from the ghetto. It is no longer a putdown. *Los Rakas* are a phenomenal Reggaeton musical group known around the world. Good guys.

Rambulera - A feisty woman with bad manners. An asshole.

Rambulería - Actions, words or gestures. *Acción, palabras o gestos desusados, antipáticos, que lleven el propósito de enojar o desagradar.*

Rambulero - A roughneck, low life. *Persona usualmente de los barrios populares que gusta de las peleas, intrigas, chismes, baile y otras manifestaciones de comunicación sin clase.*

Rándom - A person of little importance and unknown. A nobody. *Del inglés random, para referirse a una persona poco importante, desconocida o sin importancia.*

Rangálido - Looking bad. *De mal aspecto, flaco.*

Rantan - Many, a lot. *Bastante.*

Rareza - Pleasant, very good looking. *Agradable, excepcional, bonito, excelente. ¡Esos pantrlones estan rarezas!*

Rascacielos - Literally skyscrapers. Think Panama City's skyline.

Raspado *(pronunciado Raspa'o)* - 1. Shaved, flavored ice. *Hielo respado o cepillado con jugo de sabores.* 2. Scratched off lottery tickets.

Raspadura - *Jugo de caña solidificado.*

Ratita mopri awebao - Stereotypically, what rich kids call each other.

Ratona - A slut, pure and simple.

Rayos - Heck! (the exclamation). Literally lightning. *¡Rayos! Relampagos*

Ready (se pronuncia redi) - Ready. *Preparado.*

Real - A five- cent coin or a nickel. From the Spanish word for Royal*Real. Moneda de 5 centésimos de balboa.*

Recabuchar - To lust, desire, crave; have an obsessive sexual desire. *Lujuriar.*

Recula - See *Revosh*.

Redada - Dragnet. *Accion policial de detener delincuentes*

Refine - A meal, or to eat. *Comida. Refinar.*

Rejera/Pau Pau - Castigo a los hijos, ya sea darles con la correa (rejera) o con nalgadas (pau pau).

Rejero - A man who hangs out with fellow *rejeros*.

Rejeros - A group of men who hang out with other males and go out in packs to clubs and on weekends.

Rejo - Dick. *Azote, pene.*

Respet - Borrowed from rap music singers shouting out for the crowd to respect, respect. Also see: *Rispect.*

Revolincho - Children's games. *Revuelta o juegos de chiquillos o jovencitos. Los chiquillos formaron un revolincho.*

Revosh - Back up or reverse a car. *Reversa de los automoviles. Recula.*

Revulü - *Enrredo.*

Rial - 5 Cents. *Moneda de 5 centavos.*

Ricardon - - Nickname for a woman's lover. *Apodo que se le da al amante de una mujer.*

Rilax / chillin - Relax *Del inglés relax y chilling respectivamente relajado.*

Rins/rines - Car rims/wheels.

Ripiao - Caught. *Agarrado.*

Riri - See *pay*.

Rispect - Respect. *Del inglés respect usado coloquialmente como saludo de alta estima, Te mando un rispect.* See *Respet*.

Rivetiao - To dress. *Vestirse*.

Rompe pecho/manga larga - A king size bottle of beer. *Una Botella de cerveza muy grande.*

Roncabalao - A wild punch thrown without any style or technique.

Rumba - A party. *Una fiesta*

Runcho - To be of poor quality. Shoddy. Uneducated, rough. *De mala calidad. Cuando se dice de una persona, es sinonimo de inculto, basto.*

S

Saoco - Smelly. Stinky. *Ediondo*.

Sabrosón - Something you find in excellent condition. *Algo o alguien que se encuentre en excelentes condiciones o algün evento agradable. Sacalodo.*

Sacarsela - To fall. *Caerse*.

Sacar la Chucha - 1. To beat up. 2. To be involved in a really bad accident. *Sacale la chucha a ese man* - Beat that guy up *el carro se saco la chucha* - The car got all messed up.

Sae - Shortened form of the Spanish verb *saber* (To know).

Saina - A poser who tries to imitate and insinuate to give a false appearance of what actually is.

Sakakaka - A popular game, when you get hit you in the ass. Comes from *sacar* - to take out and *caca* - shit.

Salado (normalmente se dice sala'o) - Someone with bad luck. *Persona que tiene mala suerte.*

Salao - Unlucky. *Tener mala suerte.*

Salií el fulo - The sun just came out.

Sancocho - Plato tipico panameño. See prior food section.

Sapo - Accuser. *Delator.*

Sapote Chuca - In superlative. Literally, a toad.

Sarao - School dance. *Fiesta o baile organizada generalmente por el segundo ciclo de secundaria. Típicamente se realiza en horas de la tarde, en el gimnasio de la escuela. Dícese de cualquier fiesta en que el objetivo principal es bailar.*

Saraotacky - School dances held throughout the school year.

Seco - *Aguardiente.*

Secretarios - Bus driver's helper famous for instructing passengers to *Dale pa' tras* - To go all the way to the back of the bus.

Sector X - Wherever. *En cualquier lugar.*

Sencillo - A humble, unassuming person, also small money denominations, usually coins, for buying inexpensive items or paying a bus fare.

Ser un plomo - To be good for nothing.

Serruchar el piso - Literally, sawing the floor. Pulling the rug out from under. To try to push aside someone or take what belongs to him. *Robar la pareja ajena.*

Serruchón - A gossip. *Que habla mal de otras person.*

Shifear - To jilt, to avoid. *Dejar plantado, evitar. Vamos a shifear a Rodolfo para que no vaya a la fiesta. Mis compañeros de clase me hicieron un shifeo.*

Shotear - A shout out, a greating. *Saludar.*

Silampa - Drizzle. Humidity, on the cold night, dew condenses to form droplets on the ground and the grass. A creature that hides in the grey, fog. Also spelled *cilampa*.

Sin suan - A playground swing. The sound a swing makes.

Slido - Fun, fashionable, stylish This new clothing store *esta slida*.

Sobaco - Armpit. *Axilas*.

Solido - Solid. Referring to something that is cool or awesome. *Significa excelente. También, chévere.*

Sopa - In basketball, a blocked shot. Also, the puddle of sweat that forms in the underarm of a shirt. Literally, Soup.

Sopear - To sweat. *Sudar por las axilas y hacer marca en las vestimenta.*

Soplamoco - A slap a child's face. Corporal punishment. *Castigo corporal (a los niños). Te voy a dar un soplamoco a ver si te callas.*

Stick - Currency of Panama (Balboa). As in you owe me 10 sticks.

Suave - Gently, with care.

Subir - Go down, as in go down on (to fellate). *Acción de dirijirse al cuarto de una prostituta en un prostibulo.*

Surra surra - A playground slide.

T

Ta - Short for *está* (it is), as in *Ta bueno* It's good.

Ta cruel - When something is really bad, or really good. *Estí cruel*.

Tainaker - A mutt. Cur. *Perro sin raza*.

Talingo - A bothersome parrot. *Pájaro negro que no deja a las personas comer tranquilas al aire libre.*

Tallao - Well- dressed. *Bien vestido.*

Taquila - Lies. All lies. *Pura taquila.*

'Tar - To be. *Estar.*

Taradupida - Just plain dumb. *Tarada y estupida.*

Tarrantantan - Plenty. Enough. Too many. *Buco tarrantantan. Hay buco tarrantantan de hembras en la lleca.* There are too many girls in the street.

Tatai - Good- bye in baby talk originated from the Chinese language. Also, *Hasta luego, nos vemos.*

Tatequieto - A punch that leaves someone knocked out cold.

Tavuel - *Vuelta* in reverse. *Vamos a dar una tavuel,* would mean to go out (sometimes pronounced Taswel).

Tellaa - *Botella* abbreviated, a bottle of alcohol.

Temalean - Reverse of *maleante*.

Tembol (Triki) - Playground way of calling a time out. *Tiempo fuera.*

Tepesa - According to the legend, lamenting the abandonment of your children. *Frase son que segun la leyenda la llorona o la tulvieja se lamentaba por abandonar a sus hijos.*

Te voy a dar un pescozón - I am going to smack you. *Dar un golpe.*

Tiburcio - Someone absent minded or confused, with their head in the clouds. *Persona despistada o distraida.*

Tief or Teef - *Ladrone,* a friggin thief.

Tildiao - To be crazy. *Estar tildiao. Rosa y Martin estan tildiaos;* they want to move to Iraq.

Tinaco - Trash basket. Derived from *tina* or tub. *Cualquier cesto de basura. Su nombre proviene de Tin & Co., compañía que se encargaba de la recolección*

Tinakero - A mutt. *Perro que no es de razade la basura en Ciudad de*

Panamá y Colón en tiempos de la construcción del Canal de Panamá y durante mucho tiempo en Panamá que en los cestos de la basura decía el nombre de la compañía. Tinaco. Tambien se suele usar tainaker.

Tinaja - Folkloric clay pot.

Tío/tía - Respectful way to refer to an elderly person. Some *jubilados* take offense when called *abuelo/a*.

Tipo/a - Guy/Chick. Used as a noun in the same manner as guy and chick. Often times used when someone is upset when referring to that another person.

Tira lirica - Convince, persuade. *Convencer.*

Tirar la bomba de humo - *Irse de algun lugar sin que nadie se de cuenta.*

Tirar la mano - To fight. *Pelear.*

Tirar los perros - Haircut. *Cortejar.*

Tities - Small shrimp. Popcorn shrimp

To cul - It's all good.

Tof - Tough. Strong and insensitive. *1)a una persona bien fuerte, insensitiva, 2)algo de superficie sumamente dura 3) un concepto dificil de entender (Ese examen estaba bien tof.)*

Togarse - Dressed well, elegantly. *Vestirse muy finamente.*

Tongo - Policeman. Low ranking cop. *Policia de bajo rango.*

Tontón - Vagina. *El órgano sexual femenino.*

Torito - Bicho torito, a beetle. *Insecto que hace oyuelos en la tierra.*

Tortillera - Literally a tortilla maker. Disrespectful way to say gay, lesbian women.

Tospa - Pato (duck) reversed.

Tostao - Toasted. To be stoned on weed.

Totuma - *Calabazo*. Kitchen vessel made from the dried fruit of the totumo or tapara tree used by indigenous natives to carry water and take a shower. Also means a type of haircut. *Cortarse totuma* to get one's hair cut

Tranca - Lock the door.

Trancazo - A bad cold.

Tranque - Traffic jam. *Lleguí tarde por el tranqué* - I was late because of the traffic jam.

Transar - To swindle. *Estafar*.

Trepa qué sube - A very bad, difficult to solve, situation. Also known as *Arroz con mango*.

Trepaquesube/verguero/chuchamadre/zaperoco - One big problem. *Gran problema, disturbio, desorden, conflict. Encontrarse en una situación dificil de solucionar.*

Trifulca - Huge brawl. Named after Sr. Barrios de Trifulca, a newspaper columnist.

Triki triki - To call a time out. *Para pedir tiempo en algun juego.* See *Tembol*.

Trompa - Punch. *Puñetazo*.

Trozo - Vagina.

Trueno - Firearm. *Arma de fuego*.

Tubi tubi - Tubes, Hair rollers. *Enrollarse el cabello con pinzas alrededor de la cabeza para que dure más tiempo el liso del cabello despues del secado.*

Tulivieja - A witch. *Bruja*.

Tumba muerto - Tomb of death, The Ricardo J. Alfaro Avenue in Panama, Panama.

Tumbe - Rob. *Robar*.

Tuna - Carnival parade. *Desfile carnavalesco de empolleradas acompañadas de müsicos que tocan.*

V

Vaca - A collection. As in to take up a collection. *Colecta de dinero entre varias personas para comprar algo. Hey hagan una vaca pa'la Carmen ahí.*

Vaina - A thing. Stuff. *Cosa.* Often used to fill in blank spaces in conversation. *Dame esa vaina* Give me that thing. *Se cree la gran vaina.* She thinks she's the greatest thing since sliced bread. *Cosa, objeto cualquiera. Pasame esa vaina, quiero ver que es exactamente.*

Vaina loca - Crazy thing, like love.

Vale cebo - A saying that describes un unjust or stupid situation *Dícese de una situación injusta o estüpida.*

Vampira/Chupasangre - A high maintenance woman, a blood sucker. *Mujere de alto mantenimiento.*

Venao - A cuckhold. *Hombre cuya mujer le es infiel.*

Venirse - To come. To have an orgasm, to climax. *Momento cumbre del acto sexual.*

Verga - Penis. *Pene.*

Vergajo - Dick, a prick.

Vergazo - Collison, bump, bang. *Trompon.*

Verguerisidio - An issue, a big problem. *Problema bien grande.*

Vergüero - A very big problem. *Problema gran.*

Vidajena - A nosy person, a busybody. Someone who can't mind their own business, with nothing better to do than to observe and criticize others. *Tu si eres vidajena.* - You sure are nosy. *Persona que se* *dedica a observar y criticar el comportamiento ajeno.*

Vidajenear - To snoop. Too poke into the lives of others. *Interesarse, hurgar en la vida ajena.*

Vigaducto - Viaduct. An underground passage for electrical and telephone lines. *Estructura subterránea para líneas eléctricas y de telefonía.*

Violinista - A chaperone. *Persona que acopaña a una pareja pero no debe estar presente pues la pareja quiere arropar.*

Vivo - Fresh. Literally, alive.

Volao - Someone who talks nonsense. *Persona que habla tonterias.*

W

Wachimín - A security guard, or caretaker. From the English watching man. *Celador.*

Wari- wari - Creole language originating from a mixture of English, Spanish and French and spoken by the people of the Bocas del Toro province.

Waro - A cocktail, a mixed drink. *Oyé joven, traigame otro waro.* Yo, server, bring me another drink.

Washington - A dollar bill, a Balboa. *Dólar. Miguel tiene unos washingtons que podría cambiar.*

Webiando - Wasting time. *Perdiendo el tiempo.*

Wishy Washy - Windshield wipers.

X

X - *Equis*. Literally the letter X, standing for the deadly poisonous *Fer de lance viper*.

Xopa - *Paso* reversed and then *sopa's* letter S replaced with an X in order to distinguish from the word *sopa for soup*.

Y

¡Ya! - Hurry up already!

Yapla - Beach. *Reverso de playa, yaspla, y quitándole 'pla'*.

Yas - *Playa*. Letters re- ordered.

Yede - A bad smell. *Huele mal*.

Yegua - A mare.

Yeguero - Horsefucker, a sexually desperate person who will have sexual relations with anyone.

Yerbatero - An herbalist, quack doctor, *mate* dealer.

Yeyé - Stuck up, to put on airs. *Sifrino. Snobista*.

Yeyesada - Monied. Wealthy. To have *dinero. Adinerada. Persona adinerada*.

Yeyo - An illness serious enough to go require going to the doctor and missing school, or work.

Yeyooo - Greeting popular among panamanian youth, meaning everything is cool. From the singer, El Kid (Genre: Reggae, Dancehall, Roots, Rock).

Yiyinbré - Ginger bread. *Pan de jenjibre (anglicismo, derivado de* *ginger bread).*

Z

Zambito/a - Child or teenager. *Niño o niña.*

Zapatillas - Sport shoe. *Zapato deportivo para hombre o mujer.*

Zocarest o grajo - Underarm odor. *Grajobad.*

Zopilote - Turkey buzzard. Vulture.

Zorra - Trailer. Semi trailer. *Remolque.*

Zorra - Sleepy. Drowsy. *Somnolencia.*

Zoquétec - Stupid, spaced out.

A Final Word on Panamanian Spanish Versus Textbook Spanish

It should come as no big surprise to learn that Panamanians speak many of the words and phrases found in your high school and college Spanish Language books. But that said, there are some notable exceptions. Here follow a few examples of what they do and don't say on the street. Notice this section is written in Spanish, which means one needs a base level of understanding of that language in order to get any benefit from it.

El Panameño No Dice

Adinerado - *El panameño no es adinerado, sino: 1. 'ta montao. 2. Está cagado en plata.*

Afeminado - *El panameño no dice afeminado, sino maricon.*

Amigos - *El panameño no tiene amigos, sino tiene frenes, pasieros.*

Bella - *El panameño no le dice a la mujer que es bella, sino le dice que es un pay.*

Bobo - *El panameño no es bobo, sino es pendejo.*

Bocadillos - *El panameño en sus fiestas no sirve bocadillos o tapas, sino sirve picadas.*

Bolsas de plástico - *El panameño no le dan bolsas de plástico en los almacenes, sino le dan cartuchos.*

Bonito - *Para el panameño no hay algo bonito, sino hay algo solido, duro, pritty.*

Bueno - *Para el panameño, algo no esta bueno, sino esta del karajo.*

Burla - *El panameño no se burla, sino se caga de risa.*

Cachetazo - *El panameño no dice cachetazo, sino dice bofetada.*

Cacho - *El panameño no dice cacho, sino dice de cuerno.*

Cae - *El panameño no se cae, sino se saca la mierda.*

Calor - *El panameño no tiene mucho calor, sino se esta asando o cocinando.*

Carro – *1. El panameño no tiene carro, sino tiene nave. 2. El panameño no anda en un carro descuidado, sino anda rodando en una roña.*

Casa - *El panameño jamas ha tenido una casa, sino siempre ha tenido su chantin'.*

Celador - *El panameño no dice celador, sino dice wachiman.*

Cerveza - *El panameño no dice cerveza, sino: pinta, tella, encamisa.*

Chofer - *El panameño no dice chofer, sino dice palanca.*

Cigarrillos - *El panameño no dice cigarrillos, sino dice blancos.*

Confundido - *El panameño no dice estoy confundido, sino dice me guille.*

Convence - *El panameño no convence, sino tira lírica.*

Cotilleo - *El panameño no le gusta el cotilleo, sino el panameño le encanta el bochinche.*

Diarrea - *El panameño no sufre de diarrea, sino sufre de cagadera.*

Discusión - *El panameño no dice que se formó una discusión, sino que se formó un verguero.*

Distrae - *El panameño no se distrae, sino se aweva.*

Disturbio - *El panameño no dice que se formó un disturbio, sino dice se formó la chucha madre.*

Drogas - *El panameño no consume drogas, sino se vuela.*

Embotellamiento - *El panameño no está en un embotellamiento, sino el panameño está en un tranque.*

Esperma - *El panameño no dice esperma, sino dice leche.*

Excita - *El panameño no se excita, sino se entolda.*

Eyacula - *El panameño no eyacula, sino se viene.*

Fea - *Para el panameño algunas mujeres no son feas, sino son unos bagres.*

Festeja - *El panameño no sale a festeja, sino se arranca.*

Ghetto - *El panemeño no conoce el ghetto, sino conoce Bagdad.*

Golpea - *El panemeño no se golpea, sino se mete un vergazo.*

Hambre - *El panameño no tiene mucha hambre, sino 'ta pegao' o tiene buka hambre.*

Hola - *El panameño no dice Hola, te dice, sino Que Xopa.*

Homosexual - *El panameño no dice homosexual, sino dice cueco.*

Infidelidad - *El panameño no dice infidelidad, sino dice te dieron queme,* *te pasaron por la parrilla o te pusieron los cuernos.*

Lesbiana - *El panameño no dice lesbiana, sino dice tortillera.*

Licor - *El panameño no dice licor, sino dice guaro.*

Listo - *El panameño no es listo, sino es una rata.*

Lleno - *El panameño no dice que algo está lleno, sino dice está takeao, full o cojío.*

Locura - *El panameño no dice locura, sino dice ponchera.*

Masturba - *El panameño no se masturba, sino se pajea.*

Nalga - *El panameño no dice nalga, sino dice culo.*

Nino - *El panameño no dice niña o niño dice, sino dice pelaita / pelaito.*

Novia - *El panameño no tiene novia. Sino tiene Ley, Candado, Amarre, Grua, lo que sea que pueda impedir la libertad del mismo.*

Pelea - *El panameño no pelea, sino se enfrazca o se embolilla.*

Pene - *El panameño no tiene pene, sino tiene pincho, pico.*

Policía - *El panameño no dice viene la policía, sino El panameño dice viene la chota.*

Pornografia - *El panameño no ve pornografia, sino Ve Pelo Pelo.*

Puñetazo - *El panameño no dice puñetazo, sino dice: Puñete, trompada, trancaso, guabinazo o vergazo.*

Presume - *El panameño no presume, sino pifea.*

Problemas - *El panameño no dice hay problemas, sino se formó el verguero.*

Rapido - *El panameño no dice hazlo rápido, sino dice métele turbo o dale cuero.*

Reggae - *El panameño no escucha reggae, sino escucha plena.*

Romancea - *El panameño no romancea, sino arropa y se revuelca.*

Rubio - *El panameño no dice rubio o rubia dice, sino fulo o fula.*

Sale - *El panameño no sale, sino se arranca.*

Saluda - *El panameño no saluda, sino el panameño shotea.*

Tonterías - *El panameño no dice tonterías, sino, habla paja.*

Tonto - *El panameño no es tonto, sino es ahuevao'.*

Vagina - *El panameño no dice vagina: Sino dice mil cosas que no estan ni cerca a eso, dice Micha, Tonton, Chucha, Cucca, Araña.*

Verbos

Bailar - *El panameño no baila, sino el panameño tira pasos.*

Como Esta - *El panameño no dice ¿Cómo estas?, sino: ¿Qué e' lo q' e'?*

Comprar - *El panameño no dice va de compras, sino dice chopear.*

Conducir - *El panameño no conduce taxi, sino taxea.*

Dejame verlo - *El panameño no dice dejame verlo, dice pa've'.*

Disfrutar - *El panameño no disfruta de los juegos de azar, lotería, casino, o caballos, sino El panameño chinguea.*

Dormir - *El panameño no duerme, sino se hecha un sueño.*

Eres popular - *El panameño no dice eres popular, sino dice tas pegao.*

Estar bien – 1. *El panameño no dice que esta bien, sino dice que ta' cool. 2. El panameño no dice "todo esta bien," sino dice to´ta´bien*

No estar bien - *El panameño no dice algo no esta bien, sino dice esta vaina vale verga.*

Golpear - *El panameño no se golpea, sino se mete un vergazo.*

Hacer el amor - 1. *El panameño no le hace el amor a su novia, sino se la echa un polco. 2. El panameño no le hizo el amor a su mujer, sino le dio Huevo. 3. El panameño no hace el amor, sino culea.*

Ignorar - *El panameño no ignora, sino chifea.*

Juegar - *El panameño no juega, sino birrea.*

Molestar - *El panameño no se molesta, sino se cabrea, jode.*

Olvidar - *El panameño no se olvida de alguien, sino lo escracha.*

Penetrar - *El panameño no penetra a la mujer, sino se lo entierra.*

Robar - *El panameño no robar, sino transar o nachar.*

Se emborracha - *El panameño no se emborracha, sino queda hasta la verga.*

Tener buen cuerpo - *El panameño no le dice a la mujer que tiene buen cuerpo, sino dice que tiene mansa cajeta.*

Tener sexo - *El panameño no tiene sexo, sino dice culear, ponchar, o se echa' un polvo.*

No tener dinero - *El panameño no dice que no tiene dinero, sino dice que esta pelao', anda peloncho y/o anda en pelotas, anda limpio.*

Tomar siesta - *El panameño no toma siesta, sino hecha un cinco.*

Tomar traigos - *El panameño no toma, sino chupa.*

Figuras Retóricas

Enfada - *El panameño no se enfada, sino se emputa.*

Va rapido - *El panameño no va rápido, sino va a balazo.*

*El panameño **nunca pierde una discusion** porque siempre termina Mandandote pa la Vergaaaa.*

*El panameño **no pide que lo lleven,** sino, pide un bote.*

*El panameño **no dice que se formó una discusión**, sino que se formó un verguero.*

*El panameño **no anda contento y entusiasmado con un acontecimiento**, sino anda culeco.*

*El panameño **no dice que hemos comido hasta la saciedad**, sino el panameño dice: 'Toy hasta la guacha.*

*El panameño **no dice fulanito es reincidente o ésto pasó de nuevo**, sino El panameño dice vuelve y traba.*

*El panameño **no dice es una persona de clase baja y malos modales**, sino El panameño dice es una racataca, o una ratona.*

*El panameño **no dice eso se ve mal**, sino dice eso está runcho.*

*El panameño **no dice ocurrió un incidente,** sino el panameño dice se formó la vaina o la ponchera.*

*El panameño **no dice ocurrió hace poco**, sino dice pasó enante o enantito.*

*El panameño no dice **dejame verlo,** dice: Pa´ve´.*

*El panameño **no pide que lo lleven,** sino pide un bote*

El panameño no dice que **se formó un disturbio,** *sino dice se formó la chucha madre*

About the Author

Mr. Banse studied both Latin and Spanish languages in high school and university and graduated from the Defense Language Institutes' Spanish Language program. While he does not claim to be an expert linguist in any idiom, he is reasonably knowledgeable with the Spanish language in general and Panamanian slang in particular.

For more than five decades, he has enjoyed spending time in the Republic of Panama, a country he deeply loves.

While in the U.S. Army, he was stationed with the 401st Special Operations Detachment, 8th Special Forces Group (Airborne), Fort Gulick, Panama Canal Zone. One of his A-team's missions was to build a farm-to-market suspension bridge at Rio Indio, Colon province, located a few miles west of Piñas Beach, on the Caribbean Sea.

Instead of frequenting the infamous Club Siboney in Colon and slamming rum and coke, he hung out at the Panama Canal Yacht Club. There he was enthralled with the stories he heard, like the one about the Canal Zone tugboat that accidentally rammed a Chinese freighter sinking it. Or, the sad tale of the Dawn Star, a beautiful, albeit cursed, 42'-foot French-built yawl abandoned at a mooring ball in the harbor after three consecutive owners had died on board after attempting a world cruise. One of the deaths stranded a trophy wife who didn't know how to sail on the high seas. As the story goes, she survived.

The author has twice trekked the Las Cruces Trail, once in each direction. The time in the jungle lent special meaning to the stories he had read in the Fort Gulick base library about King Bayano and Cacique Comagre. Bayano was the escaped Mandinka slave who took particular delight in capturing straggling Spaniards from the mule trains and salving their thirst for gold by staking them spread-eagled on the ground and pouring ladle fulls of molten gold down their throats. It was of course Cacique Comagre (Santa María de Antigua del Darién), who told Vasco Núñez de Balboa of "the other sea," namely, the Pacific Ocean.

The author has transited the Panama Canal several times in a yacht. A dilapidated Cuban freighter lost its steering engine out of the Miraflores locks with its bow precipitously pointed straight for the

Balboa Yacht Club docks during one such transit. The author watched from onboard his sailboat as the Cuban merchant mariners dropped anchor with a cacophonous clanking and colossal cloud of rust-red dust. The only problem, the bitter end of the chain wasn't connected to a hard point, so the anchor and all of the BB chain went into the drink. Only at the last moment did the crew manage to restart the engine, crank the rudder to hard to starboard, heel over, and avoid disaster. They never stopped. The anchor and chain are still there in the muck.

With all the adventure and wonderment he experienced, it should come as no surprise to learn the author is fond of expressing his sentiment that the people and land of the Republica of Panama have melded with his soul.

"Hay un sitio en mi alma para Panama." Timothy Banse

www.ingramcontent.com/pod-product-compliance
Lightning Source LLC
Chambersburg PA
CBHW072049290426
44110CB00014B/1614